Reynolds, Bob.

Understanding derivatives.

DATE			

UNDERSTANDING DERIVATIVES

UNDERSTANDING DERIVATIVES

What You Really Need to Know about the Wild Card of International Finance

Bob Reynolds

FT
PITMAN PUBLISHING

PITMAN PUBLISHING
128 Long Acre, London WC2E 9AN

A Division of Pearson Professional Limited

First published in Great Britain 1995

British Library Cataloguing in Publication Data
A CIP catalogue record for this book can be obtained
from the British Library.

ISBN 0 273 61378 2

1 3 5 7 9 10 8 6 4 2

Typeset by PanTek Arts, Maidstone, Kent.
Printed and bound in Great Britain by
Biddles Ltd, Guildford and King's Lynn

The Publishers' policy is to use paper manufactured from sustainable forests.

To Ben Howard Leonard

my son

the finest young man in the world

LET ME EXPLAIN DERIVATIVES TRADING SIMPLY; YOU PLACE ONE BULLET IN THE CHAMBER THEN...

CONTENTS

FOREWORD

Derivatives in the headlines yet again: at the end of February 1995 the old-established British investment bank Barings sustained fatal wounds after losing £900 million on derivatives in the Japanese equities market. The nature of the speculation seems remarkable even if derivatives products were not involved. Commentators, with little apparent grasp of the basics of derivatives trading, attacked the products rather than the management of the institution.

This regrettable incident is *de facto* a consequence of the management controls of institutions dealing in derivatives rather than of the products themselves. Derivatives are risky. So management needs to put in place sufficiently resilient risk-management systems to ensure, so far as is humanly possible, that catastrophic losses do not occur. Derivatives are not inherently good or bad. Like most financial instruments they can be used to positive or negative effect. The kickback for managing them inadequately is potentially severe as we have seen in the Barings case. Whatever the inevitable enquiry will show, how was it that an individual trader became so exposed without adequate supervisory control?

As this book repeatedly says, the use of derivatives can be highly beneficial. Responsibility for extracting the best out of them lies with both traders and buyers. Traders must ensure that buyers know exactly what they are getting and what the risk profile of particular products is. Senior management at end-users must establish specific policies for risk management, setting out clearly the exposures businesses are willing to accept in respect of certain instruments and who is responsible for managing the risk.

Many of the cases which have plagued anxious corporate leaders, regulators or politicians have been driven by inadequate salesmanship or incompetent risk management. Greed has played a part – though not as much as some would have – where salespeople have chased targets or corporate treasurers pursued profit-centre as well as risk-management ambitions. And derivatives are highly suitable for both purposes. It is easy to convince unqualified buyers that a particular derivatives solution is the greatest thing since sliced bread and derivatives can make money as well as hedge successfully.

The Group of 30 has taken great steps in persuading the industry to organise itself properly and on a reputable basis. This means that traders must work to rules established and observed, mechanisms for evaluating the risk profile of products must be installed and at end-users the extent of risk which a particular culture will carry must be firmly established.

Many companies using derivatives benefit from their application. In a recent survey the *Financial Times* suggested that ten times as many customers are satisfied as are dissatisfied. The collapse of a formerly respected bank will not enhance the reputation of derivatives but in the long run it may be a good thing. This shattering blow may force traders and end-users to adopt the correct policies, procedures and risk-management systems.

Bob Reynolds
June 1995

ACKNOWLEDGEMENTS

Many thanks to: Phil Rivett and his excellent team at Coopers & Lybrand, Richard Stagg and colleagues at FT Pitman for your enthusiasm and superb support, Robert Wolfe and the Corporate Research Foundation for your kindness and enormous backing at a difficult time, Nick Baker and the *Financial Times* for the cartoons, countless colleagues in the financial media – especially Graham Hatton at the EIU, Michael Godfrey at the *Evening Standard* for allowing me to compose the derivatives feature in the paper and Michael Reynolds (no relation) for your guidance and help. Additional thanks to Artewisdom for their computer support and, last but not least, the team at Portfolio Communications for their support and great coffee.

'Most derivatives are futures instruments'

'The key phrase ... with options is: the right but not the obligation'

'Even domestic producers ... are subjected to currency risk'

1

INTRODUCTION

SUMMARY

This chapter seeks to introduce derivatives and gives an elementary understanding of how they do. It:

- **explains the function of derivatives**
- **describes the simpler types of products**
- **lists the classifications of derivatives**
- **shows how derivatives are sold**
- **identifies the main players in the industry**
- **points to the history of derivatives**

'The wild card of international finance'

'Derivatives . . . can produce spectacular financial gains'

'Speculation . . . may [explain] many derivatives-related losses'

Most of the books which cover the derivatives industry are aimed at the so-called 'rocket scientists' who devise and put together derivatives. They describe new products in language which may appear esoteric to most lay people. There is a widespread lack of understanding of derivatives – even among many intelligent managers – and part of the reason for this is the inaccessible nature of product and generic description. This book sets out to explain what derivatives are, how they operate, the function they provide, where they feature in the pattern of risk-management products, how the effectiveness of derivatives can be measured, and the various classifications of derivatives products. The onus lies not only on the dealers but also on those directors, with executive responsibility, among corporate users who have made little attempt to understand the impact that derivatives can have on their businesses.

The readership for this book is not technicians. It is aimed at those non-specialist managers and directors who need to understand derivatives because of the influence that usage of derivatives products will have on their areas of responsibility. That is why this book speaks in a consistent and straightforward voice, explaining terms and concepts in simple English. It aims to demystify derivatives and to allow the non-specialist to walk away with an appreciation of how they operate and the impact they can have. If it does that it will have succeeded.

THE WILD CARD OF INTERNATIONAL FINANCE

Derivatives have been the focus of much debate in the last few years. They are recognised as possessing the enormous capacity to be a formidable set of financial instruments. Their principal benefit is as a hedge against financial and commercial risk. It would be fair to describe derivatives as a form of corporate portfolio insurance, protecting businesses against a wide range of risks – including currency fluctuations, interest rate variations, changes in commodity prices and failures by suppliers. The potential scope of business risks is enormous, as chapter 2 of this book outlines, and therefore the opportunity such difficulties have to lead to substantial problems for individual businesses is widespread.

Discussion has centred on the proper assessment of risk associated with the products themselves. Despite the fact that derivatives have been available – albeit in their most elementary form – for more than thirty years, their extensive use has been a phenomenon of the past decade. They have been used mainly for hedging but, as the pressure on corporate treasuries to be independent profit centres has grown, there has been some degree of speculation by buyers.

Derivatives are particularly attractive because they can produce spectacular financial gains as well as giving protection. Other forms of risk management – insurance, for example – generate substantial charges while offering some protection. In contrast, derivatives can more than cover the set-up cost and so, if they are well managed, can be a potentially valuable investment.

ISSUES OF COMPLEXITY

The principal difficulty with derivatives is their complexity. Few people beyond the teams of so-called 'rocket scientists' who put them together have a thorough understanding of how they are composed and how they should be handled. Commentary in 1993 and 1994 by respected professional and industrial bodies gave gathering weight to the analysis that derivatives were intrinsically sound but that banks and end-users needed to improve considerably their understanding of the function and risk profile of derivatives.

The two main industry groups within the derivatives industry are the dealers and the end-users. Dealers either fashion derivatives specifically for particular individual clients (over-the-counter derivatives) or make available standardised contracts traded on exchanges. The world home of derivatives trading is Chicago, where the industry began in the 1950s as part of the city's extensive futures markets. The two major exchanges – the Chicago Mercantile Exchange (CME) and the Chicago Board of Trade (CBOT) – are still the world's largest derivatives arenas, although their share of the global market has become smaller since the arrival of LIFFE (the London International Financial Futures and Options Exchange) and the Deutsche Terminbörse (DTB) in Frankfurt. Exchanges in Tokyo and Sydney are also important players.

End-users can be the dealers themselves, using derivatives to protect a range of financial exposures, and buyers in the corporate and public sectors. Many companies are emphatic about the deployment of derivatives. Some are extensive users, others regard them as too complicated and find other ways to manage their business risks. Corporate losses on derivatives trading have occurred – and are covered elsewhere in this book – but for every business to experience severe losses there have been hundreds of customers who have expressed their satisfaction with derivatives products. In the last two decades the scope and application of risk-management solutions which involve derivatives have broadened extensively. The range of customers who use derivatives has widened far beyond the banks and international corporations who were the pioneers.

EXOTIC VARIETIES

Products have developed into a dizzying array of packages, many with exotic and dramatic name-tags. Cocktail swaps, barrier options, leveraged swaps, butterfly spreads, hedge funds, exploding options, strangles and straddles have joined the colourful lexicon of the markets. The simpler – 'plain vanilla' in

Products have developed into a dizzying array of packages

the terminology of the dealers – products have slowly become accepted, even conventional, instruments available to corporate treasurers to manage risk.

Another key development is the globalisation of derivatives markets. Originally, in the 1950s, financial futures exchanges were wholly US-based. In the early days, all derivatives products were exchange traded. The CBOT and the CME were the first financial futures exchanges and remain the single largest centres for derivative trading. Combined with the New York Mercantile Exchange, CBOT and CME accounted for 90 per cent of all exchange-traded derivatives until recent years. But today only half are traded in the United States. The growth of the London International Financial Futures and Options Exchange (LIFFE) and other European exchanges such as Matif in Paris and DTB in Frankfurt, coupled with expansion in Tokyo and Singapore, has spread the message of derivatives around the world. The wider world's increasing market share has been achieved notwithstanding the fact that volumes have continued to develop in the United States.

DEFINING DERIVATIVES

'Derivatives' is a portfolio term which embraces an increasing catalogue of products and product types with a staggering array of uses. The original groups of products listed as derivatives have been broadened to cover:

- new product types;
- new product classifications;
- new markets;
- new end-users;
- new kinds of risk.

The two broadest classifications of derivatives are forwards-based and options-based derivatives. There are others, which include so-called strips and mortgage-backed securities, but the two main classifications remain those identified above.

The two broadest classifications of derivatives are:
- **forwards-based derivatives**
- **options-based derivatives**

WHAT IS A DERIVATIVE?

A derivatives transaction is an agreement between two parties – known as the counterparties. Dealers and end-users overwhelmingly say that the function of a derivatives transaction is to hedge particular types of risk. These include:

- market risk;
- credit risk;
- liquidity risk.

There are many more types of risk – some are subdivisions of those listed above. For example, a company may need to borrow money but is concerned that changes in interest rates may work against it. It will use a derivatives transaction to hedge – or limit – that risk. Equally, it may put in place a derivatives solution to protect against the operational failure of its systems or production capacity.

Commodities are an important area of trading in derivatives. A producer may decide to contain its exposure to fluctuation in prices or availability of particular core materials.

There are other reasons for using derivatives, including diversification of asset allocation in an investment fund or for speculation. This second reason attracts considerable attention since it may be a core explanation of why there have been so many derivatives-related losses. Speculation is possible because derivatives can generate positive returns as well as provide risk coverage. To cover an exposure to currency risk, for example, a corporate treasury may select from a number of possibilities. Among them could be to borrow money in the cash markets or to take out a derivatives package. The first will cost money in interest rate payments. The second will cost money in terms of transaction fees but could offer financial benefits if the arrangement proves positive at its expiry.

Holders of derivatives packages may use:
- **a single transaction, or**
- **a portfolio of transactions**

Holders of derivatives packages may use a single transaction or a portfolio of transactions. A single transaction or arrangement involves the parties in a bilateral contract or payment-exchange agreement which depends on an underlying asset, reference rate or index. This asset, reference rate or index is known as the 'underlying' and can include an extensive and growing range of equities, indices, commodities, bonds and interest rates.

In a nutshell, the aim is to link an inherently unstable or unfavourable entity to one which is profoundly more stable and to produce a financial benefit. This could mean linking a basket of emerging-country currencies with a highly stable US government bond, Russian wheat futures with the price of gold or fixed-rate borrowings with floating-rate borrowings.

Derivatives are either standardised and traded on exchanges or tailor-made and sold over the counter by dealers, intermediaries or in-house specialists. The largest exchanges – Chicago and New York in the United States – account for roughly half of all worldwide derivatives transactions. London, Paris, Tokyo and Singapore now operate thriving exchanges. The biggest traders are Swiss Banking Corporation and, especially in the over-the-counter (OTC) market, Credit Suisse Financial Products, JP Morgan and Bankers Trust.

HOW DERIVATIVES ARE CONSTRUCTED

There are two main types of building blocks from which all derivatives are constructed:

Forwards are inherently simpler than options

- forwards-based derivatives;
- options-based derivatives.

Forwards-based derivatives

Forwards are inherently simpler than options. There are three main classifications of forwards:

The three main classifications of forwards:
- **forward contracts**
- **swaps**
- **futures contracts**

- forward contracts;
- swaps;
- futures contracts.

A huge volume of forward contracts is dealt daily

Forward contracts and swaps are mainly OTC products and futures contracts are largely exchanged traded. A forward contract is the simplest form of derivative. It is an agreement between two parties – one to buy and the other to sell – a nominated underlying at a specified price and date in the future. A huge volume of forward contracts is dealt daily. Particularly significant products under this classification are:

- foreign exchange forwards;
- FRAs – forward rate agreements – which are based on interest rates.

Swaps – particularly the simplest versions – are highly popular. They are relatively easy to manage and to put together. They involve an exchange of cash flows between the two parties based on an underlying instrument. The cash flows can be fixed at outset or calculated by factors in the performance of the product. There are many varieties but among the most widely used are:

- interest rate swaps;
- currency swaps;
- commodity swaps;
- equity swaps.

A typical interest rate swap may involve two companies, one of which has a better credit rating than the other. The first can therefore obtain more advantageous terms than the second. They both secure the best terms available to them in the market and then take part independently in a swap arranged by a bank. This is designed to allow both to exchange cash flows from the deal and to secure gains from the swap itself. Example 1.1 (taken from *The Financial Jungle* by Phil Rivett and Peter Speak of Coopers & Lybrand) provides a good illustration.

Futures contracts are very similar to forward contracts. The distinctions are:

- they are exchange-traded contracts rather than OTC products;
- they involve lower values than forwards or swaps and are therefore available to clients with smaller requirements;
- payment is cleared through a clearing house to limit credit exposure.

Options-based derivatives

An option is unlike any other type of financial instrument. Its functions are similar to forwards-based derivatives but it operates very differently. It derives its 'intrinsic value' from the payoff on the option at expiry plus a time element.

Example 1.1

Suppose that borrower P is an AAA rated bank which can raise fixed-rate funds at 10 per cent. However, the bank wants floating-rate debt to match its floating-rate assets. It can obtain floating-rate funds at six-month LIBOR + 0.25 per cent. Borrower Q is a BBB rated company which can raise floating-rate funds at six-month LIBOR + 0.75 per cent. However, Q wants to obtain fixed-rate debt to lock in its interest cost, but can only raise fixed rate debt at 11.50 per cent. These differences are shown below:

	Bank P	*Company Q*	*Difference*
Cost of issuing fixed-rate debt	10%	11.50%	1.50%
Cost of issuing floating-rate debt	LIBOR + 0.25%	LIBOR + 0.75%	0.50%

The net saving possible is therefore 1 per cent and a typical structure involving an investment bank acting as intermediary might be as follows:

- Bank P will issue a $100 million Eurobond on which it will pay 10 per cent fixed-rate interest. It then enters into a swap agreement involving an investment bank, under which it will pay that bank floating-rate interest at LIBOR on a 'notional' $100 million, receiving in exchange fixed-rate interest at, say, 10.3 per cent. Thus P will effectively be paying floating-rate interest at LIBOR – 0.3 per cent.
- Company Q will raise a $100 million Euroloan from a syndicate of banks and pay floating-rate interest at LIBOR + 0.75 per cent. Under the terms of the same swap agreement, Q will pay the investment bank fixed-rate interest at, say, 10.4 per cent and receive in return floating-rate interest at LIBOR. Thus Q will effectively be paying fixed-rate interest of 11.15 per cent.
- The investment bank will make 0.1 per cent (the 10.4 per cent received from Q less the 10.3 paid to P, the LIBOR payments and receipts cancelling out) as its fee for entering into the agreement.

An option is unlike any other type of financial instrument

Options are not always easy to describe but the simplest description would embrace 'the right (not the obligation), for a premium, to buy or sell an underlying instrument at the strike price during a period or on a specific date'. At heart of the option are the words 'the right (not the obligation)'. The purchaser is not obliged to exercise the right to buy or sell – it is an option. It may be in the interest of the holder *not* to exercise the right. Properly managed, with full access to appropriate risk-management systems, options can be extremely effective in handling exposures to risks which could not be covered in any other way. Again, well managed by highly capable operators, options can provide excellent hedging. But since, according to corporate treasurers, this is not a factor in their management of portfolios then it must be incidental.

The value of the option contract is linked to the volatility in the price of the underlying. The two key attributes are the call (an option to buy) and the put (an option to sell). Positions in options are described as covered or uncovered. Covered call writing (that is, selling) is the most extensively used. Four basic approaches are available to a party involved in options trading:

An option is 'the right (*not the obligation*) to buy or sell an underlying instrument at the strike price during a period or on a specific date'.

- buy a call;
- write (i.e. sell) a call;
- buy a put;
- write a put.

The range of options types and classifications is too broad to describe here but is included in chapter 6, on options products, and summarised in the glossary in chapter 10.

CORE UNDERSTANDING

Many directors or managers understand the core theory behind derivatives but find the complexities of individual products beyond them. The key to appreciating the increasing instrumental role derivatives play in the world economy is the knowledge that they form one set of tools available to manage corporate and financial risk. Risk underscores business. It is present in almost all commercial and trading activity. Managers have a repertoire of solutions available to handle the risk element in their companies – from considered inactivity, i.e. assessing that available products have greater attendant risks than the original exposure, to using multifaceted and complex packages to hedge. Derivatives products fall nearer to the latter description than to the former.

Derivatives provide a type of corporate portfolio risk insurance

Andrew Coleman at Price Waterhouse told the London *Evening Standard*: 'If company managers are seeking to hedge risk, derivatives provide a type of corporate portfolio risk insurance.' There is an element of further risk in using specific tools. In one sense it is rather like taking particular prescription drugs to cure or ameliorate a particular medical condition. They may do the job but they may also have side-effects. So it is with any risk-management product: it may provide cover for the initial exposure but at the same time create other exposures. This is how business managers and corporate advisers should earn their money – by assessing the risks and creating the best solution.

Derivatives are financial contracts between two or more parties which are based on – *derived* from – the future value of an underlying asset.

Derivatives are financial contracts between two or more parties which are based on – derived from – the future value of an underlying asset. In their most elementary form they involve swaps and options (the right – not the obligation – to buy at some future date). At their most complex they can include several interrelated units. The aim is to secure a risky investment with a more stable one . A manager at the Swiss Banking Corporation, a global top-three derivatives trader, has said:

> If you held futures in the Russian grain harvest, which at best are highly volatile, you may decide to reduce the risk by balancing them with gold futures. Derivatives make this possible and endeavour to diminish the inherent risk.

Derivatives are sold by large financial institutions – JP Morgan, Bankers Trust and Swiss Banking Corporation are placed among the global leaders – which have made extensive investment in the line and are unlikely to be surpassed. Among the global institutions is a second tier of derivatives traders, where major international banks have achieved solid positions in aspects of trading, for example, specific product areas such as swaps or options; standardised products which are traded on the principal exchanges. There is also a healthy pattern of trade by intermediary institutions. In the main the banking industry traders can be seen as a handful of global players with full service facilities, a great number of niche operators (including some which act as intermediaries) and the end-users who are the buyers. This is a highly simplistic picture but it gives some feel for the nature of the sector.

In most successful businesses leading-edge products and services, regardless of their complexity, are assessed for their market potential by managers well versed in commercial realities. Senior executives who are not 'rocket scientists' make the final decisions for the company on the relevance of new ventures. Yet directors have little appreciation of a portfolio of financial products which can often underpin the viability of an entire company or group of companies.

RISK-MANAGEMENT OPTIONS

The choice of derivatives is made – largely – because of their undoubted benefits but they form only one of a series of risk-management solutions. For all the companies and institutions which have suffered spectacular losses there are scores which continue to use – and benefit from – derivatives products. Despite the torrents of bad publicity, dealers and, more importantly, end-users who are satisfied with the contracts continue to back these products. Later in this book we look at the concept of risk management and the various methods and techniques available to institutions to hedge almost any commercial or financial risk. The rapid pace of growth in the use of derivatives owes something to fashion and more to their genuine uses.

The total value of derivatives-backed deals operating in the world shows the enthusiasm with which they have been adopted by world finance. This acceleration is demonstrated by the growth of numbers of high-value deals and also by the broadening of the applications to which derivatives are put. At the onset of the present period of increasing derivatives activity multinationals formed the vast majority of end-users. Today personal financial packages, including household mortgages and life assurance policies, are backed by derivatives instruments. This expansion will almost certainly continue apace.

Tim Plews, a partner in London's largest legal practice Clifford Chance, told the author in mid-1994 that any industry develops in stages. 'Before the derivatives sector moves into its next phase it needs to be regulated. The leading operators welcome positive regulation and have argued for changes which will give the industry greater substance.' Larger institutions want to improve the standing and performance of the sector and phase out the less reputable operators in the market.

CORPORATE IGNORANCE

If the industry adopts higher training standards the end-users can only benefit. The London *Sunday Times* reported that some salespeople have very little understanding of the products they are selling. This – along with corporate ignorance – is a key reason that derivatives achieve such a bad press. It gives politicians excellent ammunition for sniping at the industry as a whole. In the United States Congress is pressing for legislation. Demands in the United States are more pressing than elsewhere because the American industry is much larger than the others and the use of derivatives is more comprehensive in US business than anywhere else in the world. Part of their argument is rhetorical politics but some aspects reflect the genuine desire by the commercial environment to provide structure to a controversial but highly profitable industry.

Some salespeople have very little understanding of the products they are selling

However, this book is concerned with regulation and the current political debate only in so far as they impinge on the development of the derivatives industry. I have not set out to cover the twists and turns of the present dialogue.

ACCELERATING USE

Regardless of the level of debate in the United States, the heartland of derivatives, the present growth rate in their application and extension is anticipated to continue. Outside the key centres of Chicago and New York, London is the most important centre for derivatives. Relaxation of rules by the European Commission will foster an increasingly liberal environment where derivatives and other products will grow. Record Treasury Management conducted a detailed survey of the United Kingdom's finance directors. This was published as Paine-Webber, a respected US investment firm, lost $268 million on derivatives trading. The survey showed that 93 per cent of UK finance directors expect to use interest rate derivatives. Some 84 per cent were using or plan to use currency derivatives products.

93 per cent of UK finance directors expect to use interest rate derivatives

EPILOGUE

Derivatives can clearly provide considerable benefits. But their use presents many pitfalls. A most appropriate analogy was given by Richard Breeden, a Coopers & Lybrand partner, in evidence to a congressional committee:

> Derivatives, like other human inventions, can be both good and bad. For example, an automobile can provide its owner with efficient, convenient and sometimes even very pleasant transportation. However, the same model driven at 90 miles per hour down a curvy and wet mountain road may be a mortal danger to its driver and others on the road at the same time. That difference isn't the result of the car, but of how it is used. The same phenomenon is true with the use of derivatives. If the CFO or treasurer of a corporation plans to take the company's financial condition out for a drive in the markets, the CEO and the board should have a clear understanding of the plans for the journey.

Learning points

1 Derivatives are reforming the basis of financial risk transactions throughout the world but they are not new. In their simplest forms they have existed for more than thirty years.

2 Derivatives products are perceived as complex vehicles which are understood only by the financial engineers who assemble them and few others. However, the principles which guide the construction of derivatives are simple.

3 The main parties involved in derivatives transactions are dealers and end-users. Dealers are the issuing houses, mainly international banks. End-users can be the banks themselves but are more likely to be corporate treasuries.

4 Derivatives products can be simple and straightforward – even conventional – financial instruments. Equally, they can be highly complex, involving a multiplicity of interrelationships.

5 There are two main building blocks for derivatives. These are forwards-based products and options-based products. Forwards are classified into forward contracts, swaps or futures contracts. Options come in a variety of forms. What is special about options is the right – but *not* the obligation – they give the holder to buy or to sell a specified product or service at some date in the future. All derivatives involve transactions in the future.

2

THE RISKS TO WHICH A BUSINESS MAY BE EXPOSED

SUMMARY

This chapter examines risk and seeks to classify the types of risk which dealers and end-users face:

- **why and how risk is important**
- **the risks which derivatives seek to manage**
- **the risks inherent in derivatives products**
- **the risks for dealers**
- **the risks for corporate users**
- **definitions of market risk, credit risk, operational risk and legal risk**

'No business activity is without risk'

'Private capital is not alone in being at risk'

'Three-quarters of corporate treasurers . . . use derivatives to manage risk'

No business activity is without risk. Any commercial process involves a series of functions which attract different levels of risk either individually or collectively. The entirely risk-free enterprise is non-existent. One of the key skills in running a business is to identify the principal risks to which it is exposed and to manage those risks according to the objectives of its board of directors.

An essential element of this aspect of management is understanding the level of risk that the corporate culture is willing to bear. Directors should decide and regularly review the nature and extent of the risks the business is prepared to take. This is a prerequisite before examining specific types of risk and how they must be managed. Normally, attitude to risk – in the general sense – is relatively easy to define. An organisation may be risk-adverse (very conservative) or risk-orientated (willing to take a chance despite any risks involved). Pinning this down to a clear strategy is somewhat harder – but for the successful management of the level of risk inherent in ventures or activities precision is vital.

CULTURAL APPROACH TO RISK

Most successful planning for the management of business risk stems from a clear appreciation of the organisation's cultural approach to the concept of risk. Once this has been defined the preparation of risk guidelines can be achieved effectively.

Three-quarters of all corporate treasurers and almost all financial institutions say that they use derivatives to manage risk. Used effectively, derivatives and other risk-management tools can provide end-users with a coherent strategy to limit exposure and occasionally to provide financial gain. In June 1994 a columnist in the *Banker* commented: 'whether it be the

US, UK or elsewhere the real threat for the future comes from not understanding and not managing the new complexities of risk that exist today'.

Any commercial activity involves risk. It is present in any transactions where absolute certainty cannot be guaranteed, which, *de facto*, means almost every circumstance. Limiting such exposure to risk can be achieved by a range of different methods, sometimes operated singly, sometimes taken in tandem.

Among the risks which buyers and dealers of derivatives may seek to address are exposure to large swings in interest rates, minimising the cost of foreign currency or putting a limit on the price of certain commodities. For example, a corporation may borrow at a floating rate and want to fix the maximum and/or minimum levels for its debt. A government may need to use foreign currency over an extended period but want to ensure that the cost can be contained.

Any commercial activity involves risk

ENCOUNTERING RISK

In the January 1995 *Harvard Business Review* one of its authors gave examples of the types of risk which a business could face:

- fluctuations in short- or long-term interest rates;
- currency exchange rates;
- oil prices;
- equity market levels.

This is not an exhaustive list but it goes some way toward defining the breadth of risks commonly encountered by businesses:

> By managing financial risks well, companies can improve their flexibility and adaptability in managing the other sorts of business risks that cannot be avoided. A risk management programme

should reduce a company's exposure to the classes of risk it is not in business to take while reshaping its exposure to those it is.

Phil Rivett of Coopers & Lybrand classifies the range of business risk accordingly:

> There are many risks to which a business can be exposed. There is no such thing as a risk free business. For example, a UK manufacturer of computer hardware which sells its products in dollars may be subject to a potential disadvantage from currency rate exposure. A US publisher relies on his profit in future years on the sale of books. A significant cost element is the paper on which to print his books. The profit (or even loss) may be influenced by the cost of pulp in Finnish or Canadian markets. Commodity prices may rise steeply and thus he may run the risk of significant reduction in profit potential.

There is no such thing as a risk free business

Many grades of risk can be encountered. Among them are:

- exchange rate risk;
- interest rate risk;
- commodity price risk;
- equity price risk;
- market risk;
- credit risk;
- operational risk;
- legal risk;
- liquidity risk.

The first four are directly price-sensitive. A business may be at a disadvantage if any of these prices turn down. The remaining five are discussed in more detail later in the chapter but, for conven-ience, are briefly described below.

Market risk arises when market factors cause a change in the price of goods or services (and thus includes the first four).

Credit risk occurs, quite simply, if a customer fails to meet his or her financial obligations for the supply of goods or services.

Operational risk could involve, for example, the malfunctioning of a crucial piece of production technology, a downturn in systems, a failure in distribution channels or a strike by employees.

Legal risk – axiomatically – is the risk that an activity by a company may lead to legal action against it. For example, an oil company transports crude oil by tanker. If a ship runs aground and spills its cargo the owner could be sued by the country whose coastline has been despoiled.

Liquidity risk arises where mismatches in cash inflows and outflows leave insufficient cash to meet current obligations.

ARE WE IN THE RIGHT LINE?

Governing all these types of risk is an umbrella concept which may be termed suitability risk. This involves asking major questions about the purpose and conduct of business. The test of suitability risk can be applied at either a macro or micro level. The principal suitability risk question, regardless of the scale of the subject of the test, is: 'Should we really be in this business at all?' This can be asked in the context of an entire enterprise. A high-tech manufacturing company may look at the market and compare the competition's strengths with its own. Its directors may decide that rivals are too strong and have the capacity to sustain and grow profits. In the absence of any special factors – producing a revolutionary new chip, say, or adding radical new features – this conclusion may make them consider that their market is not a suitable place in which to operate.

A German electronics company may examine the suitability of a particular market segment. It may be selling CD systems to consumers over the age of fifty in north-east Germany. This may not be a core market; it may indeed be one where competitors have achieved better results. The risks of staying in this market may be too great for any forecast return.

THE BIGGEST RISK OF ALL

Finally, there is also systemic risk. This is the nightmare of all regulators. Since derivatives, intrinsically, link weak products with strong ones, regulators fear that a run on a weak product could destabilise strong ones. The stock market crash of 1987 is thought to be due in part to the linkages created by derivatives. This, combined with programmed trading, pulled down the entire market.

Systemic risk ... is the nightmare of all regulators

Systemic risk could impact a specific market sector – or, at worst, result in a collapse of whole areas of the world's markets. Given the instantaneous transmission of information systemic risk could happen too quickly to regain manual control.

THE RISKS RUN BY DIFFERENT TYPES OF ORGANISATION

Banks

Typical risks for banks include:

- default on commercial loans;
- failure by borrowers to meet interest terms;
- currency fluctuations;
- interest rate changes;
- failure to understand the dynamics of a particular customer or corporate business.

Commercial businesses

Currency fluctuation

In the corporate environment, businesses may need to hedge against currency fluctuation (see Example 2.1).

Example 2.1

ABC Enterprises Inc. in the United States enters into a contract to supply machine parts to a German car manufacturer, who insists on a fixed price for the three-year deal. Over that time the value of the order may suffer from variations n the relationship between the dollar and the mark. ABC therefore attempts to find the most cost-effective way of protecting the contract value against negative currency fluctuations. There are many devices by which the US company can protect itself against this eventuality. Many options, including derivatives, may also offer a financial bonus if the 'insurance policy' is unnecessary.

In addition, ABC depends on a second-tier supplier to provide components for the machine parts it intends to supply to its German client. ABC may also wish to take out some kind of financial protection in case the supplier fails to meet its target in any terms, for example quality standards or timeliness. (Businesses deal daily with these sorts of risk in order to remain competitive and to try to prepare for any eventuality which may threaten fulfilment of commercial obligations.)

Asset exposure

Balance sheet financial exposures occur in current assets, for example:

- Is the level of current assets high compared with total assets? If so, why?
- The nature of the portfolio of marketable securities – are all investments denominated in the company's accounting currency?
- What is the relationship between the company's long-term debt and its cash and marketable securities position?
- Are there currency exposures in the company's inventory?

Exposures are also apparent in fixed assets. Among the questions which should be asked are:

- Where are the fixed assets?
- What sales do they support – local or foreign?
- Is asset replacement likely?

Equity exposure

In the investment area of the balance sheet there may be equity exposures. 'Equity exposures are a fact of life for a large number of firms,' commented *Risk Magazine*'s *Guide to Corporate Exposure Management*. 'A company that suffers write-downs on its portfolio may incur unfavourable tax or accounting consequences.'

The guide points to key areas of concern regarding equity investments including:

- Are there any investments which place significant capital at risk?
- Overseas investments may be subject to risk in themselves or in the way that they are funded.

Debt exposure

In the debt portfolio, financial exposures could occur in relation to:

- the ratio of fixed-rate to floating-rate debt, net of financial products such as swaps and forwards;
- convertible bonds, debts with warrants or the like, which certainly contain additional financial exposures which need to be managed.

Competitive exposure

In the competitive arena other exposures emerge. These include:

- the currencies in which competitors are exposed;
- whether rivals hedge some or most of their financial risks;
- are competitors' commodity exposures denominated in dollars or local currency?

Risk Magazine commented:

> Competitive exposures – no less real than other exposures – present a particular identification problem, because they are more difficult to quantify than are exposures on the balance sheet. It is one thing to say that a German firm competing with a Japanese firm has an implicit long position in the yen, it is another to determine the amount of exposure to be hedged.

A RULE OF THUMB FOR DISCUSSING RISK

For ease of discussion most operators consider risk in terms of five types. These are the areas where day-to-day issues emerge:

- market risk;
- credit risk;
- operational risk;
- legal risk;
- liquidity risk.

Market risk

Market risk occurs when the prices of goods or services change because of market factors. It is important to investigate the components of the market risk and understand how they interrelate. When dealing with risk-management tools, it is vital to assess the so-called mark to market valuation of products and the underlying instruments used as hedges.

Credit risk

Credit risk is the risk of loss due to the other party defaulting on a contract.

This is the risk that a loss will occur if the other party defaults on a contract. Indeed, a business may well decide a company is not creditworthy and therefore too much of a risk to engage with in trading. Conversely, it may regard the credit standing of a potential client as sufficiently good to conduct business with.

Market risk occurs when the prices of goods or services change because of market factors.

The degree of credit risk will vary according to the different constituents of an agreement. Factors which might suggest greater credit risk:

- significant exposure to individual parties in total and for settlement on any given day;
- significant volumes of high-yielding instruments issued by lower-rated companies and banks.

The credit risk of transactions varies in time and nature with the rating of the counterparty/client. In assessing credit risk, two questions need to be asked:

- If the counterparty defaulted today, what would be the cost of replacing the transaction?
- If a counterparty should default at some stage in the future, what is a reasonable estimate of the potential replacement cost?

Potential exposure

Assessing the potential cost of replacing a transaction at some future date can be difficult. Any potential risk can be judged on past experience or by using simulation models.

Operational risk

Operational risk – as the name implies – covers the risk of running a business and may occur in, among others, the following aspects of a business:

- inadequate systems;
- insufficient management control;

- human control;
- various degrees of management failure.

'Operational risk' covers the risk of running a business. It could include criminal acts by employees or directors.

It could even include criminal acts intended to obtain an illicit benefit from the business's resources, like fraud by an employee or a director, or industrial espionage or sabotage by a competitor.

These risks occur principally in manufacturing enterprises but they can also be seen in action in securities and credit businesses.

Checklist: How to check up on your risk profile

The key areas of control include:

- **overseeing senior management control**
- **checking documentation of policies and procedures, listing approved activities and establishing precise objectives, credit controls and management reports**
- **providing independent risk-management functions**
- **delivering independent internal audits**
- **ensuring that an effective back-office system exists**
- **putting in place internal checks and balances at all stages of risk-management activities**

Legal risk

This occurs primarily when a company encounters the risk of punitive legal action through default on a contract. Risk here can arise from:

- insufficient documentation;
- insufficient capacity;
- uncertain legality;
- unenforceability following bankruptcy or insolvency.

Legal risk – axiomatically – is the risk that a company's activities may lead to legal action being taken against it.

In addition to contract risks, legal risk arises in other ways. The example of a grounded oil tanker was given earlier. Equally, a tobacco company runs the risk that smokers may sue it for, in their view, failing to warn them of any potential health risks in consuming its products. Alternatively, one company may sue another for failure to provide certain components on time (a straightforward contract breach), leading to the loss of an order.

Liquidity risk

With derivatives, two forms of liquidity risk arise:

- that due to inadequate market depth, or market disruptions, a company may be unable to (or may only with difficulty) unwind or offset a position it has taken at or near to the previous market price;
- that a company's cash-flow position simply leaves it unable to meet payment obligations on, for example, settlement dates.

RISK PROFILE

The Basle Committee on Banking Supervision and the Technical Committee of the International Organisation of Securities Commissions published an excellent summary to define risk profile, the various types of risks and the management of risk. The relevant parts of its report are reproduced in Appendices I and II at the end of the book.

Learning points

1 Risk is a factor inherent in all business and trading activities.

2 Companies need to decide the level of risk which culturally they are willing to bear.

3 The nature of financial and operational risk can include: exchange

rate, interest rate, commodity, equity and operational risk – all price risks; legal and credit risk.

4 A company may also choose to assess 'suitability risk'. This is the suitability of everything that concerns the company – from a product in a particular market to the relevance of being engaged in key sections of the business.

5 Systemic risk may also be a concern. This is where one market failure impacts on other areas of the economy and causes a general collapse.

6 The main classifications of risk are: market risk, credit risk, operational risk, liquidity risk and legal risk. (The management of these risks is outlined in chapter 3.)

7 The set of guidelines (given in the checklist in the chapter) for examining the risk profile of a particular company should be understood and applied.

3

WAYS TO MANAGE THE FINANCIAL RISK

SUMMARY

This chapter gives a general description of some of the techniques for identifying and then managing financial risk:

- **doing something or doing nothing**
- **the reasons for doing nothing**
- **the reasons for doing something**
- **the types of exposure which should be managed**
- **the benefits of managing exposure**
- **the groups which benefit from management of exposure**

'businesses encounter many different forms of risk'

'reducing the volatility of cash flows provides reassurance'

'[suitability risk] is mainly cultural'

As we saw in chapter 2, businesses encounter many different forms of risk. There exists a range of possibilities for the management of that risk and in this chapter we look at ways businesses might approach this situation.

SOMETHING OR NOTHING

After studying the risks and making a plan, a company may decide to do nothing. The important question to ask here is: Is this decision *conscious* or *unconscious*? That is: have you considered all the options and decided that doing nothing is the best way forward?

The reasons for doing nothing might include:

- the risks involved in any strategy to manage the perceived existing business risks are greater than the original exposure;
- the cost of managing the risk is greater than any financial penalty which the original risk can reasonably be expected to incur;
- on balance, the identified risk is insufficiently great to expend management time and resources.

'Flying naked in the wind' is highly risky in itself, particularly if it is solely reactive rather than a coherent, well-formed strategy. The dangers of doing nothing are legion. It can, however, be the most appropriate approach if all the factors are considered – and on balance, after due reflection, it is deemed the most effective way forward. In this case, doing nothing is making a positive decision to do *something*.

> ***'Flying naked in the wind' is highly risky in itself***

The only alternative course of action is, *de facto*, to do something. 'In one way or another this approach is to alter the way in which you do business,' says Coopers & Lybrand partner Phil Rivett.

The key factor in managing business risks is to identify the type of risk and seek appropriate ways of handling that particular exposure. Having decided that a risk must be actively managed, a strategy for 'hedging' the risk can be developed. Hedging involves using policies to limit or offset a particular risk. Derivatives are the most well-known products for hedging. The objective is to contain risks by providing financial coverage to ensure that any exposure can be managed.

Among the types of exposure which companies may wish to manage are:

- interest rate exposure;
- currency exposure;
- commodity exposure;
- credit exposure;
- equity exposure.

The normal rationale for managing such exposures is that by developing a strategic approach to a particular business problem (or problems) considerable value can be added to the company. Stated simply, the market value of a business is the net present value of its anticipated cash flows. This means that, potentially, that value can be altered only by changing one or more of the following factors:

- tax liabilities;
- cash flows;
- the discount rate charged to the company.

Such means of stabilising cash flows, enhancing investment and cash-flow planning, allow businesses to concentrate on the primary risks and increase the benefits of debt financing.

Stabilising cash flows

When a business's risks are managed so as to stabilise its cash flows, the benefits appear in several ways. For example:

- Companies with more stable cash flows may trade at a premium to their more volatile peers.
- Hedging is an excellent way of managing and thus stabilising cash flows. It:
  - is cost effective;
  - avoids earnings surprises.
- Income will probably be sufficient to service debts. This reduces the likelihood of bankruptcy or failure.

Improving cash flow and investment planning

Hedging enables companies to avoid being caught up in the vicious cycle that starts with deferring investment when cash flows fall. This can produce less than quality investment results in the long term. Management which goes for the long-term view inevitably boosts the value of the company.

Focusing on primary business risks

Hedging helps to unbundle risks and exchange less controllable ones for those which the company has a marked capacity to handle. *Risk Magazine*'s *Guide to Corporate Exposure Management* cites an airline which wants to hedge against fuel price increases and therefore separates out oil prices from the running of the business. Equally, an oil company's management may increase its exposure to the fluctuations in the oil market. This is because the company is perceived to be very good at managing this risk.

Hedging is an excellent way of managing and thus stabilising cash flows

Increasing the advantages of debt finance

Reducing the volatility of cash flows provides reassurance to bondholders that the company will not default. Thus, the credit rating of the business should improve and its debt capacity increase.

Extending the benefits of exposure management

The shareholders in a business are the main beneficiaries of managing exposure but there are other groups who are also helped by corporate exposure policy. The nature of the exposure and the extent to which these different groups are assisted by policy in this area vary enormously.

- *Creditors* have a fixed claim on the business. They have an interest in active management to decrease risks to the business. A policy here can add reassurance.
- *Employees* also exert a fixed influence on cash flows in terms of increased profitability leading to improved employment prospects and conditions.
- *Customers* can be exposed to considerable fluctuations of price in the company's goods and services. It is thus in the interests of the business to manage the risks effectively.

THE KEY AREAS OF RISK AND HOW TO MANAGE THEM

The Basle Committee/IOSCO guidelines (referred to in chapter 2) define the types and areas of risk to which businesses using derivatives will be exposed, and make a number of recommendations in relation to them. These are reproduced in Appendices I and II at the end of the book. From a self-regulatory point of view, the Derivatives Policy Group has also published a report, and the relevant portion appears in Appendix III.

CURRENCY EXPOSURES

Currency exposure may result in a company borrowing proportionally in each of several currencies. A corporation with assets denominated in dollars may fund those assets in dollars too. On the plus side, this helps currency control and diversifying interest rate exposure, but, on the minus side, impedes unbundling interest rate from currency exposure.

Risk Magazine comments:

> A more strategic operating solution is to select production sites in overseas markets, entering either by means of acquisitions or of setting up a new facility. For example, a Japanese firm competing in the United States market will be at a competitive disadvantage relative to US competitors so long as the yen is strong against the dollar; that is, the Japanese firm has a long dollar position on the revenue side of the income statement. One solution would be to set up operations within the United States, which would establish a long dollar position on the cost side as well. The solution would have certain economic advantages not directly related to currency exposure: if transport costs are a significant component of the price of the firm's output, for example, there would be economic advantages to choosing production sites closer to the market. And if the US market is protected by tariffs or quotas, there would be few alternatives to direct entry.
>
> But the operating solution would also expose the firm to costs connected with the US market, such as labour and real estate costs and regulatory compliance costs. In addition, a firm must consider not only the costs of entry to a market; if the firm's strategy changes it must consider the costs of exit as well. Many costs of entry, such as legal and regulatory costs, are sunk once incurred and cannot be recovered when leaving; further, divestiture is likely to involve declines in the value of assets acquired to make the initial investment in the market. Finally, there may be economies of scale

Establishing overseas operations to manage currency exposure is a blunt instrument

in producing in one facility that would be lost if production were dispersed among two or more facilities. Again, locating overseas would help control currency exposures but at the price of higher unit costs of production. In summary, establishing overseas operations to manage currency exposure is a blunt instrument because it involves bundled costs and risks which are not easily separable.

Learning points

1 There are several different approaches that businesses can take to the management of risk.

2 A strategic approach to risk management is the most intelligent way forward.

3 After assessing the risks inherent in a particular commercial venture management may decide to take any one of a number of different courses of action.

4 Doing something or even doing nothing may be the option selected but that choice should be arrived at after due consideration.

5 The option of doing nothing may be appropriate if the cost of introducing a hedge is more expensive than the exposure. Equally, the extent of the risk may be so small as not to warrant any action.

6 If the decision to act is made, benefits will follow from any hedging decision. The introduction of a strategic plan to hedge will bring greater stability.

7 Derivatives are but one of several possible solutions to the problem of handling the risk.

4

DERIVATIVES

SUMMARY

This chapter examines the nature and application of derivatives:

- **background to the development of derivatives**
- **the reasons for using derivatives**
- **corporate investment in former derivatives traders to manage treasuries**
- **definition of derivatives**
- **distinction between exchange-traded and over-the-counter derivatives**
- **the building blocks of derivatives: forwards and options**
- **the forms forwards and options take**
- **who uses derivatives**
- **functions of dealers and end-users**

‘Every business needs to expose itself to risk in order to seek profit’

‘Some corporations have recruited leading derivatives traders . . . to provide their treasuries with professional expertise’

‘the concept underpinning derivatives is simple, . . . flexible and powerful’

In the previous chapters we have looked at the nature of risk and approaches to managing it successfully. Among the range of risk-management tools available are derivatives. In January 1995 the *Harvard Business Review* told its readers: 'the use of derivatives has become popular in recent years as corporations look for new and better ways to manage financial and operating risks'. It went on to comment that 'financial decisions that were previously designed and implemented by specialists [need] to be monitored more closely from the very top of the organisations'.

One of the authors of the article commented:

> derivative instruments are no more than tactical tools – albeit very valuable ones for implementing risk management strategies. Every business needs to expose itself to risk in order to seek profit. But there are some risks which a company is in business to take on and some that it is not.
>
> Consider the case of airline that has an opportunity to buy the rights to serve a new route from Chicago to London. The expected return on equity might be about 25 per cent but the chance of an outright loss might be 35 per cent. This is the type of risk that an airline is in business to take, even if the fear of losing money keeps its executives awake at night. However the top management might be able to reshape the risk by selling an investor an option on a share of the profits from the route. The additional income from the sale of the option might be enough to lower the probability of outright loss to say, 10 per cent, while the expected return on equity might fall to only 20 per cent.

This neatly encapsulates a typical scenario. In the language of the currently fashionable aspects of management science, a business has core competences. Taking a normal business risk on those core competences is part of commercial life but the extent of possible failure could be substantially reduced without undermining earnings.

Risk Magazine's *Guide to Corporate Exposure Management* gives a further typical example:

> Competitive currency exposures can arise at the operating cost line when a company has an advantageous cost position. A company exporting to Japan has a short position in the dollar (and a long one in the yen) because it benefits from a depreciation of its home currency relative to the yen by becoming more competitive in the Japanese market. For example, in the mid-1980s Caterpillar's competitiveness suffered because of the strength of the dollar relative to the yen, which enabled Komatsu to gain a competitive edge. Even companies that operate only in their domestic market have currency exposure to the extent that their competitors operate in countries with depreciating currencies. The effects of currency changes can be complex. For example, a US-based steel producer may find that the weak dollar improves export opportunities. But the finished goods into which the steel goes, such as foreign-built autos exported to the US may be less competitive at their destination.

These are only two of the typical exposures against which derivatives seek to hedge. As mentioned in chapter 3, there are many situations which will create risk that a business will want to manage. Properly used, derivatives are flexible instruments which adapt to many business risks and offer a return in addition to their principal function as hedging products.

INCOMPLETE UNDERSTANDING

Recent losses which have been widely reported in the financial press come from an incomplete understanding of the way the products work and their risk profile. A report in November 1994 issued by Record Treasury Management said that although 90 per cent of the company directors who were surveyed used derivatives, more than half of them thought that the banks' salespeople were not properly briefed on their risks. Only 1 per cent thought that banks were good at explaining such risks.

More than half . . . thought that the banks' salespeople were not properly briefed on their risks

Corporate treasurers, the report concluded, were equally in the dark. They may not be doing enough to monitor or manage their derivatives risks effectively. Despite the volatility in financial markets, treasurers were 'marking to market' – checking the value of their holdings – less frequently than the accepted industry standard. Record's chief executive Les Halpin told the *Financial Times* that they 'should have the facility to mark to market on a daily basis'. Yet only 16 per cent were running such exercises daily. More than three-quarters of the sample 'mark to market' their derivatives exposures no more than once a month or less often.

The report goes on to reveal that despite the significant losses of recent months companies continue to operate their treasuries as profit centres. Although three-quarters of corporate treasurers regard derivatives primarily as risk-management tools, 10 per cent of the group believe that they can add value. This means that they may have taken on risks unrelated to their ordinary business activities.

Halpin continued: 'Nearly one in ten see themselves as profit centres. That is enough to give you all the disasters you need for the next 20 years.' The survey suggested that more management resources should be directed toward derivatives monitoring. And board-level directors should be better informed about the risk-management policies of their companies. Nearly half of the respondents required board approval for commitments of above £1.5 million but one in five make decisions about derivatives transactions of £50 million and above without recourse to the board.

A SPECIALIST'S ART

Richard Lapper's piece in the International Capital Markets section of the *Financial Times* quoted Record's chairman, Neil Record: 'Treasurers tend to see derivatives as a do it yourself business. In other areas of business where specialist expertise is needed, like accounting and the law, companies appoint outside advisers.'

At the end of September 1994 the Bank of International Settlements in Geneva concluded in a report that derivatives risk is completely misunderstood. 'The standard method to compute a maximum credit loss is essentially meaningless.' In contrast, Robert Benson, head of Midland Bank's derivatives team based in London, told the London *Sunday Times*: 'We have had a bad press because people who lost a lot of money find it easier to blame the instruments rather than look at their own judgements.'

Dealers' criticism is directed towards corporate managers and directors who do not understand derivatives and their impact. They suggest that within treasuries managers are ill-equipped to make correct investment decisions which use derivatives. The banks tend to steer away – at least publicly – from internal analysis which would indicate that their own salespeople and senior directors are as guilty as their customers.

As a counterpoint it is worth pointing out that the Group of 30 1993 report which was designed to stay the hand of regulators did recommend improved training. The G30 report was compiled by a study group funded by the larger and, in the main, more responsible traders. Its members included Bankers Trust, Swiss Banking Corporation, Goldman Sachs, Credit Suisse, Merrill Lynch, Bank of Tokyo and Salomon Brothers. It was co-ordinated by Dennis Weatherstone, chairman of one of the world's largest derivatives traders JP Morgan. At a time of increasing pressure by regulators the report made a significant contribution to the debate. One of its aims was to indicate how a framework for regulation could be devised which would lay to rest some of the more persistent complaints about derivatives management. But at the same time the point was made that derivatives would not be stifled and that they could continue to make a considerable contribution to the world economy.

As the industry has developed over the last twenty to twenty-five years so awareness has improved. Some corporations have recruited leading derivatives traders in an attempt to provide their treasuries with professional expertise. Directors of some businesses have taken the trouble to learn about derivatives.

However, most of the really spectacular derivatives-related collapses have occurred during the last eighteen months to two years. And products are becoming harder to unravel. In October 1994 James Bethell wrote in the London *Sunday Times*: 'not only are the instruments becoming more intricate and the deals spanning more markets . . . but trading desks are increasingly focusing on long-term positions, where the matrices of financial factors can be mind-bogglingly complex'.

KEY GROUPS WHERE IGNORANCE IS PREVALENT

The key groups where ignorance is most prevalent are therefore:

- the banks' and financial institutions' salespeople;
- bank directors;
- corporate treasuries;
- company boards.

Many salespeople do not understand their products and cannot advise buyers/end-users of the real risks involved. Bank directors tend to leave the intricacies of derivatives to the 'rocket scientists' and to their managers, without understanding or evaluating the implications for and exposure of their institutions. Corporate treasurers are guilty of thinking they understand the impact of their decisions using risk-management techniques when they do not. Company directors, like their counterparts in the institutions, appear to delegate responsibility for massive areas of exposure to managers.

Many salespeople do not understand their products

The level of understanding is elementary. Derivatives activity continues to grow apace in volume, nature and scope of end-user, the number of institutions which use derivatives to back personal products, and portfolios of instruments. Yet dissatisfaction persists. In part it is the pattern of that concern which has fuelled the demand for this book. This chapter examines what derivatives are and how they work.

A DEFINITION

The most effective description of derivatives was included in the report of the G30 study published in September 1993:

> In general terms, a derivatives transaction is a bilateral contract or payment exchange agreement whose value depends on – derives from – the value of an underlying asset, reference rate or index. Today, derivatives transactions cover a broad range of underlyings – interest rates, exchange rates, commodities, equities and other indices.
>
> In addition to privately negotiated, global transactions, derivatives also include standardised futures and options on futures that are actively traded on organised exchanges and securities such as call warrants.
>
> The term derivative is also used by some observers to refer to a wide variety of [other] instruments . . . [These] have payoff characteristics [which reflect the fact that they include derivatives products as part of their make-up] . . .

'In general terms, a derivatives transaction is a bilateral contract or payment exchange agreement whose value depends on – derives from – the value of an underlying asset, reference rate or index.'

[The majority of trades are in over-the-counter (OTC) products:] those privately negotiated contracts provided directly to end-users, as opposed to the standardised contracts (futures) sold on exchanges. The main OTC derivatives include swaps, forwards and options, based upon interest rates, currencies, equities, and commodities.

Through derivatives, the complex risks that are bound together in instruments can be teased apart and managed independently, and often more efficiently. For many that issues securities and for many that invest, derivatives can save costs and increase returns while broadening the range of funding and investment alternatives.

Table 4.1 lists typical derivatives contracts and securities and, where appropriate, identifies (in square brackets) the exchanges where they are traded. Table 4.2 lists the principal exchanges. While the range of products is diverse it is not as complicated as it appears at first sight. Every derivatives transaction is constructed from two simple building blocks that are fundamental to all derivatives: forwards and options. They include:

- *Forwards*: forwards and swaps, as well as exchange-traded futures.
- *Options*: privately negotiated OTC options (including caps, collars, floors and options on forward and swap contracts), exchange-traded options on futures.

Every derivatives transaction is constructed from two simple building blocks

Diverse forms of derivatives are created by using these building blocks in different ways and by applying them to a wide assortment of underlying assets, rates or indices.

Table 4.1 Typical derivatives contracts and securities

Privately negotiated forwards (OTC)	Forward commodity contracts Forward exchange contracts Forward rate agreements (FRAs) Currency swaps Interest rate swaps Commodity swaps Equity swaps
Privately negotiated options (OTC)	Commodity options Currency options Equity options FRA options Caps, floors, collars Swaps options Bond options
Exchange-traded futures	Eurodollar [CME] US Treasury bond [CBOT] 9% British gilt [LIFFE] CAC-40 [Matif] DM/$ [IMM] German Bund [DTB] Gold [Nymex]
Exchange-traded options	S&P futures options [Nymex] Bond futures options [LIFFE] Corn futures options [CBOT] Yen/$ futures options [IMM]
Structured securities and deposits	Dual currency bonds Commodity linked bonds Yield curve notes Equity linked bank deposits
Stripped securities	Treasury strips IOs and POs (interest-only/principal-only contracts – usually related to mortgages)
Securities with option characteristics	Callable bonds Putable bonds Convertible securities Warrants

Table 4.2 Principal exchanges and the common abbreviations

Amex	American Stock Exchange
AOM	Australian Options Market
ATA	Agricultural Futures Exchange Amsterdam
Belfox	Belgian Futures & Options Exchange
BM&F	Bolsa Mercadorias & de Futuros
CBOE	Chicago Options Exchange
CBOT	Chicago Board of Trade
CME	Chicago Mercantile Exchange
CRCE	Chicago Rice & Cotton Exchange
DTB	Deutsche Terminbörse
EOE	European Options Exchange
Finex	Financial Instrument Exchange
Futop	Guarantee Fund Danish Options & Futures
FOM	Finnish Options Market
HKFE	Hong Kong Futures Exchange
IPE	International Petroleum Exchange
KCBT	Kansas City Board of Trade
Kanex	Kansai Agricultural Commodities Exchange
LIFFE	London International Financial Futures and Options Exchange
LCE	London Commodity Exchange
Matif	Marché à Terme International de France
Meff RF	Meff Renta Fija
MIF	Mercato Italiano Futures
MGE	Minneapolis Grain Exchange
Meff RV	Meff Renta Variable
MidAm	MidAmerica Commodity Exchange
Monep	Marché des Options Négociables de la Bourse de Paris
NYCE	New York Cotton Exchange
NYFE	New York Futures Exchange
Nymex	New York Mercantile Exchange
NZFOE	New Zealand Futures & Options Exchange
OM	Stockholm Options Market
OMLX	London Securities & Derivatives Exchange
Osaka	Osaka Securities Exchange
OSE	Oslo Stock Exchange
Otob	Austrian Futures & Options Exchange
PHLX	Philadelphia Stock Exchange
Safex	South African Futures Exchange
SFE	Sydney Futures Exchange
Simex	Singapore International Monetary Exchange
Soffex	Swiss Options & Financial Futures Exchange
TIFFE	Tokyo International Financial Futures Exchange
Tocom	Tokyo Commodity Exchange
Toronto	Toronto Stock Exchange
TGE	Tokyo Grain Exchange
TSE	Tokyo Stock Exchange
WCE	Winnipeg Commodity Exchange

A BRIEF HISTORY

Beverly Chandler's book *Managed Futures* gives a thoughtful history of the futures markets. She argues that the ancestral lineage of derivatives can be traced back at least four hundred years – and possibly more – to the early London commercial markets.

The recent history of futures trading began in Chicago in the early 1970s when the first financial futures were created. Chicago remains the home of futures and derivatives and in 1994 almost 500 million futures and options contracts were traded at the city's three exchanges: the Chicago Board of Trade, Chicago Options Exchange and Chicago Mercantile Exchange. The London International Financial Futures and Options Exchange handled 100 million contracts. The other major international trader is the New York Mercantile Exchange.

Tracy Corrigan, in the *Financial Times* in 1993, summarised the rapid explosion in exchanges worldwide and indicated that in the United States markets had achieved a phase of reduced growth.

> Twenty years ago futures exchanges were viewed as quirky offshoots of larger markets. Although still treated with suspicion in some quarters, futures exchanges have now positioned themselves at the heart of the world's financial markets.
>
> The notional amount of futures traded annually is now estimated at $140,000 billion. The growth of the futures markets has been fuelled by increasing sophistication and internationalisation of financial markets, including the proliferation of complex OTC products which are then hedged using exchange-traded products.
>
> The rapid development of financial markets in the past 20 years could arguably not have been realised without the growth of futures and options exchanges. The establishment of futures contracts has been an important factor in ensuring liquidity and hedging opportunities. The new techniques developed in the derivatives market have had an impact on investment management, trading, technology and risk management.

She argued that in the United States the futures market appears to be developing into maturity. Although exchanges outside America are continuing to grow rapidly, especially in the United Kingdom, Brazil, France and Germany, in the United States margins are shrinking, competition is intense and market share is being lost to the Europeans. Although Europe is enjoying a 40 per cent annual volume growth in many exchanges, it faces its own problems. Jorg Franke, chairman of the Deutsche Terminbörse, told Corrigan that with more than twenty exchanges trading in derivatives products Europe has more than it needs.

The notional amount of futures traded annually is now estimated at $140,000 billion

GROWTH IN DERIVATIVES PRODUCTS

The International Swaps and Derivatives Association (ISDA) survey data provides the most comprehensive information to measure the level, growth and composition of OTC derivatives activity. Measurement of the scope of derivatives trades has always been a nightmare because of double counting – where both sides of each deal are counted – so ISDA data is adjusted to take account of this factor.

Tables 4.3 to 4.6 show the market activity in the following sectors: interest rate and currency swaps, interest rate options, and equity, commodity and multi-asset derivatives.

Table 4.3 shows that the notional principal of interest rate plus currency swaps written in 1991 was $1.95 trillion. That represented an increase of 32 per cent over 1990 and a fourfold increase since 1987. The notional principal of interest rate swaps during 1991 was £1.62 trillion, again over four times that in 1987. Currency swaps in 1991 generated $328 billion, slightly less than three times the figure for four years earlier.

Table 4.3 Interest rate and currency swaps written annually by underlying and outstanding 1987–91 (Notional principal in US$ billion)

Type of swap	*1987*	*1988*	*1989*	*1990*	*1991*
Interest rate swaps					
US$	287	366	545	676	926
DM	22	33	41	106	103
Yen	32	43	62	137	194
Others	47	126	185	345	399
Subtotal	388	568	833	1,264	1,622
Currency swaps					
Yen–dollar	24	35	53	48	80
Others–dollar	30	35	40	33	60
Non-dollar	32	54	86	132	188
Subtotal	86	124	179	213	328
Total swaps written	474	692	1,012	1,477	1,950
Total swaps outstanding (at year-end)	867	1,328	1,952	2,890	3,872

Source: International Swaps and Derivatives Association

Table 4.4 Interest rate and currency swaps written annually by type of counterparty and outstanding 1987–91 (Notional principal in US$ billion)

Counterparty	*1987*	*1988*	*1989*	*1990*	*1991*
Transactions between dealers	144	222	368	546	865
Transactions with end-users					
Financial institutions	203	282	370	472	591
Corporations	86	127	186	286	362
Governments	35	52	63	98	111
Others	6	9	25	75	21
Subtotal	330	470	644	931	1,085
Total swaps written	474	692	1,012	1,477	1,950
Total swaps outstanding (at year-end)	867	1,328	1,952	2,890	3,872

Source: International Swaps and Derivatives Association

Table 4.4 shows swap activity by counterparty. Some 44 per cent of interest rate and currency swaps were transactions between dealers, 30 per cent between dealers and financial institutions, 18.6 per cent between dealers and corporations and 5.7 per cent between dealers and governments.

Table 4.5 shows the composition of interest rate options by type of option – cap, floor, collar or swaption. The total notional principal of these newer derivatives options was $578 billion at year-end 1991. Caps grew by 25 per cent over two years to $317 billion. Floors stood at $129 billion, up 50 per cent on 1989. Collars chalked up $23 billion, which was 41 per cent less than 1989. Swaptions experienced substantial growth, with a 50 per cent increase on 1989 to reach $109 billion.

Table 4.5 Interest rate options: caps, floors, collars, and swaptions outstanding 1989–91 (Notional principal in US$ billion)

Year-end	*1989*	*1990*	*1991*
Caps			
US$	177	251	225
Non-US$	77	68	92
Subtotal	254	319	317
Floors			
US$	54	76	73
Non-US$	32	34	56
Subtotal	86	110	129
Collars			
US$	35	33	13
Non-US$	4	5	10
Subtotal	39	38	23
Swaptions			
US$	51	63	57
Non-US$	21	31	52
Subtotal	72	94	109
Combined			
US$	317	423	368
Non-US$	134	138	210
Total	451	561	578

Source: International Swaps and Derivatives Association

Table 4.6 looks at year-end 1992 information on equity, commodity and multi-asset derivatives. Gathering this information was a new activity for ISDA. Equity swaps brought in $10 billion, equity options $66 billion, commodity swaps $18 billion, commodity options $12 billion and multi-asset transactions $25 billion. The total amount is $131 billion.

Table 4.6 Equity commodity, and multi-asset derivatives outstanding at year-end 1992 (Notional principal in US$ billion)

	Transactions between dealers	*Transactions with end-users*	*Total outstanding*
Commodity swaps			
Energy	5	10	15
Metals	–	3	3
Subtotal	5	13	18
Commodity options			
Energy	2	3	5
Metals	2	5	7
Subtotal	4	8	12
Equity swaps			
Indices (by index country)			
Japan	3	3	6
US	1	1	2
Other	–	1	1
Baskets and individual stocks	–	1	1
Subtotal	4	6	10
Equity options			
Indices (by index country)			
Japan	11	9	20
US	3	8	11
UK	6	5	11
Germany	4	2	6
France	3	2	5
Other	2	2	4
Baskets	–	2	2
Individual stocks	1	6	7
Subtotal	30	36	66
Multi-asset transactions	10	15	25
Combined total	53	78	131

Source: International Swaps and Derivatives Association

Table 4.7 then lists the top fifteen derivatives exchanges and the top ten for equity options. Finally, in the appendix to this chapter, a number of tables are brought together to show the variety (and volume) of derivatives transactions.

Table 4.7 The top derivatives and equity options exchanges by volume of transactions

Position	*Exchange*	*Jan–Jun 94*	*Jan–Jun 93*
Derivatives exchanges			
1 (1)	CBOT	121,697,633	83,214,433
2 (2)	CME	117,206,937	73,797,969
3 (3)	CBOE	92,436,199	69,426,077
4 (4)	LIFFE	87,231,866	45,522,354
5 (5)	Matif	56,994,926	32,739,454
6 (6)	BM&F	42,843,042	27,881,800
7 (10)	DTB	33,814,306	15,595,656
8 (7)	Nymex	29,730,513	24,834,980
9 (8)	Amex	24,907,615	19,485,684
10 (11)	LME	22,871,191	15,038,229
11 (13)	TIFFE	21,226,143	10,460,993
12 (9)	Pacific	19,516,698	15,743,238
13 (14)	SFE	16,973,373	10,401,479
14 (–)	Soffex	14,489,064	8,320,024
15 (12)	PHLX	13,357,148	12,948,637
Equity options			
1 (1)	CBOE	36,421,553	26,355,066
2 (2)	Amex	23,079,537	17,006,045
3 (4)	Pacific	9,706,081	7,723,268
4 (3)	Soffex	9,538,064	8,137,845
5 (6)	PHLX	6,256,147	5,884,493
6 (7)	Australian Opts	5,864,257	3,709,023
7 (5)	DTB	5,575,470	5,954,732
8 (9)	OM	4,421,158	2,428,923
9 (8)	EOE	4,140,830	3,430,996
10 (10)	LIFFE	2,386,773	2,349,478

Source: *Futures and Options World*

WHO USES DERIVATIVES?

While the concept underpinning derivatives is simple, it is also flexible and powerful. The G30 report describes the action of derivatives thus:

> a party exposed to an unwanted risk can pass that risk to another party and assume a different risk or pay cash in return. For example, in a swap transaction, two parties with reciprocal risks can reduce or eliminate them by exchanging payment streams. A borrower can, in effect, exchange payments on a debt in Swiss francs for an obligation in US dollars. An investor can exchange the return on a basket of US stocks for the return on a basket of German stocks. A buyer of petroleum can fix the price of future purchases in Japanese yen, Deutsche marks or many other currencies.

The development of products which can be described as derivatives has been prompted by explicit market need. The principal function is hedging. Specific needs include:

- tools to manage risk;
- the search for higher yields;
- lower funding costs.

The broader and more general needs include:

- diverse and changing needs of a wide array of users;
- hedging current and future risks;
- taking market risk positions;
- exploiting inefficiencies between markets.

The concept underpinning derivatives is simple

Derivatives users are divided into two categories: dealers and end-users. Dealers, typically, are mainly banks and securities houses, with some insurers and highly rated corporations (mainly in the energy and motor sectors). End-users comprise corporations, government entities, institutional investors and financial institutions. There is clearly a degree of overlap. An institution may participate in derivatives both as a dealer and as an end-user. A money-center bank (that is, one of the major US banking corporations) acts as an end-user when it uses derivatives to hedge its asset and liability management. As a dealer, it may quote bids and offers and commit capital to meet customer demand for derivatives. Both dealers and end-users, via derivatives, can manage separately risks and other characteristics present in conventional financial instruments.

Selected combinations of cash flow, interest rate, currency, liquidity and market source charateristics can be treated separately, each independent of the underlying instrument. So managers can respond to fundamental risks.

Specific users

End-users

The reasons end-users select derivatives include the following: to hedge, lower funding costs, to enhance yields, to diversify sources of funding and to reflect market views through position taking.

The G30 report identified corporations as key end-users. For its 1993 document the study group commissioned a survey of industry practice. More than 80 per cent of corporations considered derivatives very important or imperative for controlling risk. Roughly 87 per cent of the respondents use interest rate swaps, 64 per cent use currency swaps and 78 per cent use forward foreign exchange contracts. Among options-based derivatives, 40 per cent use interest rate options and 31 per cent currency options.

Governments and public sector bodies have particular requirements as well. Some needs are very similar to those of non-financial corporations. The use of swaps by organisations like the World Bank can be traced back for many years. The highly publicised deal between IBM and the Bank in 1981 is still a landmark – due to the sheer size and volume of contracts – in the growth of governments' use of derivatives. The US federal government's agencies like the Federal National Mortgage Association and the Student Loan Marketing Association are regular risk-management users of derivatives. Numerous local authorities, including Washington DC, Atlanta, Boston, San Francisco and Delaware, cap or lock-in fuel costs as part of energy policy.

The use of swaps by organisations like the World Bank can be traced back for many years

Institutional investors have long utilised asset swaps to enhance yield through arbitrage. They use interest rate and equity swaps to manage exposure to debt and equity markets. As end-users, more than 83 per cent of financial institutions find derivatives very important or imperative in managing risk. Some 92 per cent use interest rate swaps, 54 per cent take FRAs, 46 per cent favour currency swaps, 85 per cent use cross-currency rate swaps and 69 per cent choose forward foreign exchange contracts. In addition, 69 per cent select interest rate options and 23 per cent feature currency options.

Dealers

The G30 provides an instructive description of dealers:

> Early in the evolution of OTC derivatives, financial institutions acted for the most part as brokers finding counterparties with offsetting requirements on notional amount, currencies, type of interest to be paid, frequency of payments and maturity. They negotiated on behalf of the two parties. Acting as agent or broker, the institutions took no principal position in the transactions and were not exposed to credit or market risk.
>
> They soon found their role evolved beyond brokering into dealers, offering themselves as counterparties or principals to immediate customer requirements.

The next step involved 'warehousing'. Dealers would temporarily hedge a swap until a matched postition could be found.

Most dealers today operate a portfolio approach. A dealer takes a customer's transaction into its portfolio or book of derivatives transactions and manages the net or residual portion of the overall position. This means that dealers are better able to manage the entirety of their customers' transactions. Also they can monitor and manage the various components of market risk.

Other functions of dealers include:

- liquidity and continuous availability of transactions;
- meeting the demands by end-users for immediacy;
- providing the capacity to enhance market liquidity and price efficiency.

Learning points

1 Derivatives are widely used throughout the world by banks and companies in an increasingly surprising array of circumstances.

2 These products are tools to enable users to manage risk more effectively. They are also used for speculation.

3 The level of understanding of the risk inherent in derivatves, especially by corporate treasuries – and of the systems to manage that risk – is deeply inadequate.

4 The key groups of derivatives users are banks, financial services groups and companies. The principal participants are traders and end-users.

5 A derivative is an agreement between two to parties to buy or sell a product or a service at some date in the future. The value of the contract derives from an underlying asset.

6 Financial futures were originally created in Chicago. They spread to other exchanges, first in the United States and now around the

world. There are two forms: exchange-traded derivatives and customised, over-the-counter (OTC) products.

7 All derivatives are constructed from two building blocks: forwards-based products and options-based products.

8 Derivatives may be sold as individual products or in portfolios.

Appendix: Variety and volume of derivatives

The sheer variety of high-performing contracts and novel products is illustrated by this selection of data from *Futures & Options World*'s 1994 review. We are grateful to them for permitting us to reproduce the data. (For the abbreviations, see table 4.2. In these tables 'f'= forwards-based, 'o' = options-based contracts.)

Table A1 New contracts

Contract	*Exchange*	*Volume*	*Date*
3-mth Krona; IMM-FRA	OM	1,860,971	2 April
Int-rate swap (non guar)	BM&F	1,831,685	22 March
German Bobl future	LIFFE	1,049,640	21 January
IGBM Inflation index futures	BM&F	258,375	30 July
S&P Depository Receipts	Amex*	500,000	29 January
Bel-20 Index options	Belfox	345,510	2 April
Hang Seng Index options	HKFE	295,220	5 March
Flex options	CBOE	288,179	26 February
Maof 25 Index options	TASE	125,000	1 August
MBB2 bond	OM	182,721	14 April
Int-rate x exch rate (no guar)	BM&F	3,850	3 December
5-Yr Govt bond	Matif	99,260	17 June
Mibor 360	Meff	44,130	1 October
Wilshire Small Cap Ind Op	PSE	153,007	11 January
$/DM deferred spot	Simex	26,298	1 November
Mortgage credit bond	Futop	28,618	25 October
CBOE & S&P sector indices	CBOE	89,456	24 May
Three month Cibor	Futop	34,727	22 September
10-yr JGB futures	Simex	29,253	1 October
MSCI HK index futures	Simex	80,466	31 March
Int-rate swap (guaranteed)	BM&F	77,412	22 March
DM Rollng spot	CME	28,936	14 September
$/Yen deferred spot	Simex	13,182	1 November
10-Yr Govt bond	Otob	43,410	9 July
Bel-20 Index futures	Belfox	11,970	29 October
French franc futures	CME	19,343	20 September
Option on Bobl future	DTB	62,976	15 January
DRG Leaps index options	Amex	42,894	12 April
No 7 raw sugar	LCE	14,202	1 October
Int-rate x exch-rate (guar)	BM&F	3,850	3 December
10-Yr Govt bond futures	OSE	28,245	18 June
Euromark futures	CME	26,058	26 April
Flex options	Amex	8,300	9 October
Gold futures	BM&F	11,720	27 August
Spanish Govt bond futures	LIFFE	28,318	10 March
Long treasury bond futures	Matif	24,768	28 January
30-Yr bond; ops on int-rate	CBOE	4,477	5 November
Russell 2000 Index futures	CME	19,479	4 February
Exchange rate swap	BM&F	1,437	3 December
10-Yr treasury note futures	MidAm	11,615	30 April
3-Yr Govt bond futures	NZFOE	10,545	14 May
Soybean futures	BM&F	7,375	16 July
Overnight 10-Yr bond	SFE	2,082	15 November
Euromark options	CME	8,923	26 April
10-Yr note; ops on int-rate	CBOE	598	5 November
Shrimp futures	MGE	1,437	12 July
Sterling rolling spot	CME	1,277	15 June
Nonfat dry milk futures	CSCE	1,276	15 June
Overnight 3-Yr bond	SFE	320	15 November
Utility Index options	NYSE	307	15 November
Wilshire Small Cap Index futures	CBOT	1,626	11 January
Russell 2000 Index options	CME	1,428	4 February
Dollar composite index futures	CBOT	733	4 June
5-Yr note; opts on int-rate	CBOE	186	5 November
Five day copper options	Comex	534	10 August
Cheddar cheese futures	CSCE	669	15 June
Shrimp options	MGE	465	12 July
Sterling rolling spot options	CME	254	15 June
Nonfat dry milk options	CSCE	296	15 June
Eurotop 100 index options	Comex	533	8 January
Cheddar cheese options	CSCE	174	15 June
Oat options	MGE	177	1 April
BTK Leaps index option	Amex	230	7 June
Midwest Catastrophe insurance	CBOT	74	7 May
5-Yr Treasury note future	MidAm	39	30 April
NYSE Utility Index futures	NYFE	10	15 November

*1 trading lot = 100 Spiders

Table A2 Top contracts

Position		*Contract*	*Exchange*	*1993*	*1992*
1	(1)	US T-bond	f CBOT	79,428,474	70,003,894
2	(3)	Eurodollar	f CME	64,411,394	60,531,066
3	(2)	S&P 100	o CBOE	64,031,944	62,427,272
4	(4)	Notionnel	f Matif	36,804,824	31,082,844
5	(5)	Crude oil	f Nymex	24,868,602	21,109,562
6	(6)	US T-bond	o CBOT	23,435,164	20,258,740
7	(7)	3-mth Euroyen	f TIFFE	23,386,958	14,959,373
8	(9)	Dax	o DTB	21,419,890	13,944,986
9	(14)	3-mth Euromark	f LIFFE	21,318,942	12,173,431
10	(11)	German Bund	f LIFFE	20,440,442	13,604,523
11	(8)	Interest rate	f BM&F	18,996,117	14,072,749
12	(10)	Eurodollar	o CME	17,008,764	13,762,628
13	(19)	10-yr T-note	f CBOT	16,601,258	11,217,938
14	(12)	S&P 500	f CBOE	16,454,282	13,420,174
15	(16)	10-yr JGB	f TSE	15,126,159	11,868,127
16	(30)	Copper	f LME	14,855,430	7,338,242
17	(13)	S&P 500	f CME	13,204,413	12,414,157
18	(17)	Deutschemark	f CME	12,866,451	11,593,174
19	(18)	3-mth Sterling	f LIFFE	12,135,981	11,296,327
20	(24)	Long gilt	f LIFFE	11,808,998	8,804,639
21	(–)	Pibor	f Matif	11,803,798	6,430,780
22	(23)	Soybeans	f CBOT	11,649,333	9,000,169
23	(21)	Notionnel	o Matif	11,572,671	10,047,391
24	(20)	Corn	f CBOT	11,462,618	10,356,632
25	(–)	Ibex 35	f Meff	10,843,599	2,872,197
26	(–)	Ibovespa	f BM&F	10,374,860	7,287,054
27	(25)	Aluminium	f LME	10,083,342	8,225,792
28	(28)	Gold	o BM&F	9,406,163	7,932,576
29	(–)	Gold	f Comex	8,916,195	6,002,009
30	(–)	Brent crude	f IPE	8,852,549	6,172,155

Table A3 Top interest rate contracts

Position		*Contract*	*Exchange*	*1993*	*1992*
1	(1)	US T-bond	f CBOT	79,428,474	70,004,799
2	(2)	Eurodollar	f CME	64,411,394	60,531,066
3	(3)	Notionnel	f Matif	36,804,824	31,082,844
4	(4)	US T-bond	o CBOT	23,435,164	20,258,740
5	(5)	Euroyen	f TIFFE	23,386,958	14,959,373
6	(9)	Euromark	f LIFFE	21,318,942	12,173,431
7	(8)	German Bund	f LIFFE	20,440,442	13,604,523
8	(6)	Cruzeiro Int-rate	f BM&F	18,996,117	14,072,628
9	(7)	Eurodollar	o CME	17,008,764	13,762,628
10	(–)	10-Yr T-Note	f CBOT	16,601,258	11,217,938

Table A4 Top currency contracts

Position		*Contract*	*Exchange*	*1993*	*1992*
1	(1)	Deutschemark	f CME	12,866,451	11,593,174
2	(6)	$ Cruzeiro	f BM&F	7,608,631	4,474,117
3	(2)	Deutschemark	o PHLX	6,217,792	7,966,240
4	(5)	Yen	f CME	6,023,132	4,520,356
5	(3)	Deutschemark	o CME	5,916,463	6,354,248
6	(4)	Swiss Franc	f CME	5,604,841	5,134,717
7	(–)	French Franc	o PHLX	3,978,929	1,261,319
8	(7)	British Pound	f CME	3,701,427	3,053,428
9	(8)	Yen	o CME	2,261,977	1,518,409
10	(10)	Canadian Dollar	f CME	1,410,818	1,171,640

Table A5 Top futures exchanges (excluding equity and cash options)

Position		*Exchange*	*1993*	*1992*
1	(1)	CBOT	178,773,105	150,030,460
2	(2)	CME	146,746,990	134,238,555
3	(3)	LIFFE	93,668,252	65,872,355
4	(5)	Matif	72,263,961	55,474,238
5	(5)	Nymex	55,412,436	47,212,417
6	(6)	BM&F	52,263,719	34,231,094
7	(7)	LME	35,289,932	24,741,869
8	(10)	TIFFE	24,121,713	15,540,487
9	(9)	SFE	21,481,096	17,557,685
10	(–)	Comex	18,854,113	12,731,179

Table A6 Top equity options

Position		*Exchange*	*Equity options* 1993	1992
1	(1)	CBOE	58,710,818	44,968,235
2	(2)	Amex	38,341,443	36,067,822
3	(3)	Pacific	16,347,224	13,034,947
4	(8)	Soffex	13,399,813	5,902,300
5	(5)	DTB	12,252,791	9,996,329
6	(4)	PHLX	11,411,065	10,262,430
7	(7)	Australian options	9,509,891	6,551,025
8	(6)	EOE	7,629,684	6,631,120
9	(10)	OM	7,068,099	3,543,240
10	(9)	LIFFE	4,767,093	4,571,669

Table A7 Top stock indices

Position		*Contract*	*Stock indices Exchange*	*1993*	*1992*
1	(1)	S&P 100	o CBOE	64,031,944	62,427,272
2	(2)	Dax	o DTB	21,419,890	13,944,986
3	(3)	S&P 500	o CBOE	16,454,282	13,420,174
4	(4)	S&P 500	f CME	13,204,413	12,414,157
5	(–)	Ibex 35	f Meff	10,843,599	2,872,197
6	(8)	Ibovespa	f BM&F	10,374,860	7,287,054
7	(5)	Nikkei 225	o Osaka	8,461,458	11,927,329
8	(6)	Nikkei 225	o Osaka	6,090,375	9,256,981
9	(–)	CAC 40	f Matif	5,908,739	3,601,476
10	(7)	SMI	o Soffex	5,595,388	7,794,024

Table A8 Half-year performance January to June 1994

Position		*Contract*	*Exchange*	*Jan-Jun 94*	*Jan-Jun 93*
Top contracts					
1	(1)	US T-bond f	CBOT	55,914,665	38,736,260
2	(3)	Eurodollar f	CME	54,770,703	32,284,480
3	(2)	S&P 100 o	CBOE	41,079,033	34,527,491
4	(4)	Notionnel f	Matif	31,363,785	17,452,147
5	(10)	German Bund f	LIFFE	21,713,991	9,081,679
6	(8)	3 mth Euroyen f	TIFFE	20,900,020	10,065,704
7	(7)	3 mth Euromark f	LIFFE	17,286,232	10,651,273
8	(6)	US T-bond o	CBOT	15,869,451	10,794,092
9	(9)	Interest rate f	BM&F	14,830,194	9,428,154
10	(11)	Eurodollar o	CME	14,282,458	8,900,731
11	(–)	Ibex 35 f	Meff RV	14,280,072	3,683,132
12	(5)	Crude oil f	Nymex	14,016,081	10,926,661
13	(12)	Dax o	DTB	12,869,626	8,355,234
14	(13)	10 yr T-note f	CBOT	12,855,375	8,005,551
15	(16)	S&P 500 f	CBOE	12,711,850	7,970,659
16	(–)	Long gilt f	LIFFE	11,847,936	4,824,480
17	(–)	Notionnel o	Matif	10,984,160	5,197,371
18	(16)	S&P 500 f	CME	9,153,178	6,775,393
19	(19)	3 mth Sterling f	LIFFE	8,437,058	5,807,764
20	(–)	Gold f	Tocom	8,317,437	2,840,409
Stock indices					
1	(1)	S&P 100 o	CBOE	41,079,033	34,527,491
2	(7)	Ibex 35 f	Meff RV	14,280,072	3,683,132
3	(2)	Dax o	DTB	12,869,626	8,355,234
4	(3)	S&P 500 o	CBOE	12,711,850	7,970,659
5	(4)	S&P 500 f	CME	9,153,178	6,775,393
6	(10)	CAC 40 f	Matif	4,066,142	2,558,602
7	(–)	Ibex 35 o	Meff RV	3,910,890	1,624,897
8	(5)	Ibovespa f	BM&F	3,791,983	5,374,992
9	(9)	SMI o	Soffex	2,988,875	2,644,539
10	(6)	Nikkei 225 f	Osaka	2,985,037	4,805,475
Currencies					
1	(3)	$Cruzeiro f	BM&F	6,519,867	3,291,030
2	(1)	Deutschmark f	CME	6,107,408	6,575,812
3	(6)	Yen f	CME	3,499,301	2,715,216
4	(5)	Swiss Franc f	CME	2,762,460	2,869,129
5	(4)	Deutschmark o	CME	2,749,216	3,169,931
6	(8)	French Franc f	PHLX	2,524,899	1,325,872
7	(2)	Deutschmark o	PHLX	1,927,836	3,747,144
8	(7)	Sterling f	CME	1,902,599	1,732,775
9	(9)	Yen o	CME	1,667,614	898,187
10	(–)	$ Canada f	CME	861,579	589,329

Position		Contract	Exchange	Jan-Jun 94	Jan-Jun 93
Interest rates					
1	(1)	US T-bond f	CBOT	55,914,665	38,736,260
2	(2)	Eurodollar f	CME	54,770,703	32,284,480
3	(3)	Notionnel f	Matif	31,363,785	17,452,147
4	(8)	German Bund f	LIFFE	21,713,991	9,081,679
5	(6)	Euroyen f	TIFFE	20,900,020	10,065,704
6	(5)	3 mth Euromark f	LIFFE	17,286,232	10,651,273
7	(4)	US T-bond o	CBOT	15,869,451	10,794,092
8	(7)	Interest rate f	BM&F	14,830,194	9,428,154
9	(9)	Eurodollar o	CME	14,282,458	8,900,731
10	(0)	10 Yr T-Note f	CBOT	12,855,375	8,005,551
Metals					
1	(5)	Gold f	Tocom	8,371,437	2,840,409
2	(1)	Copper f	LME	8,252,276	6,135,282
3	(3)	Aluminium f	LME	7,121,151	4,522,808
4	(4)	Gold f	Comex	4,707,469	4,215,964
5	(2)	Gold o	BM&F	4,390,874	5,017,393
6	(7)	Silver f	Comex	3,359,193	2,160,066
7	(6)	Platinum f	Tocom	2,934,207	2,274,903
8	(8)	Zinc f	LME	2,614,790	1,727,778
9	(–)	Nickel f	LME	1,571,349	971,110
10	(10)	Copper f	Comex	1,408,713	987,744
Grains					
1	(2)	Corn f	CBOT	6,975,634	4,558,097
2	(1)	Soybean f	CBOT	6,229,882	4,809,464
3	(3)	Red beans f	TGE	2,536,522	3,123,151
4	(5)	Soybean oil f	CBOT	2,421,384	1,989,193
5	(4)	Soybean meal f	CBOT	2,380,356	2,114,057
Meats					
1	(1)	Live cattle f	CME	1,836,143	1,705,112
2	(2)	Live hogs f	CME	753,230	766,592
3	(3)	Pork bellies f	CME	354,587	395,656
4	(4)	Live cattle o	CME	272,259	274,605
5	(5)	Feeder cattle f	CME	236,957	205,511
Energy					
1	(1)	Crude oil f	Nymex	14,016,081	10,926,661
2	(2)	Brent crude f	IPE	5,007,655	3,986,837
3	(3)	Heating oil f	Nymex	4,712,821	3,800,041
4	(4)	Unleaded gas g	Nymex	3,764,041	3,399,064
5	(5)	Crude oil o	Nymex	3,090,739	3,294,372
Softs					
1	(1)	Sugar No 11 f	CSCE	2,459,335	2,643,186
2	(3)	Coffee C f	CSCE	1,585,471	1,272,183
3	(2)	Cotton f	Tocom	1,497,630	1,347,491
4	(4)	Cocoa f	CSCE	1,281,222	816,267
5	(5)	Cotton f	NYCE	1,270,945	813,607

5

FORWARDS-BASED DERIVATIVES

SUMMARY

This chapter describes one of the two principal divisions of derivatives products – forwards-based derivatives:

- **a description of forwards-based derivatives – forwards contracts, swaps, futures contracts**
- **how forwards, swaps and futures operate**
- **descriptions of the main types of these products**
- **examples of FRAs, swaps and futures in operation**

'The simplest form of derivatives is the forward contract'

'In April 1992 . . . daily trade in forward contracts was . . . $420 billion'

'FRAs are used by anyone who . . . desires to hedge or limit [interest rate] risk'

THE PRINCIPAL CLASSIFICATIONS OF DERIVATIVES PRODUCTS

Derivatives are divided into two principal classifications. This chapter and chapter 6 provide a guide to how these are structured and the nature of that structure. The control functions for forwards and options are discussed in chapter 7.

FORWARDS-BASED DERIVATIVES

There are three divisions of forwards-based derivatives:

- forward contracts;
- swaps;
- futures contracts.

The forward contract

The simplest form of derivatives is the forward contract. It obliges one party to buy, and the other to sell, a specified quantity of a nominated underlying financial instrument at a specific price, on a specified date in the future. There are markets for a multitude of underlyings. Among these are the traditional agricultural or physical commodities, currencies (foreign exchange forwards) and interest rates (forward rate agreements – FRAs). The volume of trade in forward contracts is massive. In 1993 the Bank of International Settlements published a survey of foreign exchange market activity. It drew on figures from April 1992. At that moment daily trade in forward contracts was quoted as being $420 billion. Growth has since continued apace.

The three forwards-based derivatives:
- **forward contracts**
- **swaps**
- **futures contracts**

The change in value in a forward contract is broadly equal to the change in value in the underlying. Forwards differ from options in that options carry a different payoff profile. Forward contracts are unique to every trade. They are customised to meet the specific requirements of each end-user. The characteristics of each transaction include the particular business, financial or risk-management targets of the counterparties. Forwards are not standardised. The terms in relation to contract size, delivery grade, location, delivery date and credit period are always negotiated.

A forward contract obliges one party to buy, the other to sell, a nominated underlying at a specific price, quantity and date in the future.

In a forward, contract the buyer of the contract draws its value at maturity from its delivery terms or a cash settlement. On maturity, if the price of the underlying is higher than the contract price the buyer makes a profit. If the price is lower, the buyer suffers a loss. The gain to the buyer is a loss to the seller.

Swaps

A swap transaction commits the participants to exchange cash flows at specified intervals, which are called payment or settlement dates. Cash flows are either fixed or calculated for specific dates by multiplying the quantity of the underlying by specified reference rates or prices.

The vast majority of swaps are classified into the following groups:

- interest rate;
- currency;
- commodity;
- equity.

The notional principal (i.e. the face value of a security) on all these, except currency swaps, is used to calculate the payment stream but not exchanged. Interim payments are usually netted – the difference is paid by one party to the other.

The main users of swaps are large multinational banks or corporations

Like forwards, the main users of swaps are large multinational banks or corporations. Swaps create credit exposures and are individually designed to meet the risk-management objectives of the participants.

Futures contracts

A basic futures contract is very similar to the forward contract in its obligation and payoff profile. The volume of newer financial futures contracts in interest rates, currencies and equity indices now far outstrips the original markets in agricultural commodities.

There are some important distinctions between futures and forwards and swaps.

- The contract terms of futures are standardised. These encompass:
  - quantity and quality of the underlying;
  - time and place of delivery;
  - method of payment.

  The only variable is the price. Even the credit risk is standardised: this is greatly reduced by marking the contract to market on a daily basis with daily checking of position.

Futures . . . are available to a wider business market

- Futures are smaller in contract size than forwards and swaps, which means that they are available to a wider business market.

We now look at how these various products work.

FORWARD RATE AGREEMENTS (FRAs)

An FRA contract sets the interest cost on a particular amount on a specified date in the future. The following are its key features.

- Its principal does not exchange hands since it is notional only.
- A contract is settled in a single payment, being the difference between the interest rate featured in the contract and the market rates (also indicated in the contract). The payment is made, on a discounted basis, at the start of the contract.
- Parties conclude their agreements either directly or through a broker rather than on an exchange.
- It can be written to cover any future period, any currency or any amount. FRAs are often described as tailor-made or OTC futures contracts.

FRAs are used by anyone – bank or corporate treasurers – who is exposed to interest rate risk and desires to hedge or limit that risk. As they use notional principal only, they are off-balance-sheet items. So they are particularly popular with banks interested in managing the scope of their balance sheets.

The main centres for FRAs are New York and London, where major US and UK banks are the key operators in the interbank market in FRAs. The US dollar is the principal denominating currency but there are busy markets in sterling, yen, Deutschmarks, Swiss francs and Australian dollars. Two years after its inception in 1984 the notional outstanding principal was $10 billion. Most of the deals in the FRA market are interbank and are contained within a period of one year. Longer-term contracts are, however, available.

The process of a transaction involves either the buyer or seller of an FRA asking the writer – usually a bank – for a quote. The buyer expects a rise in interest rates, the seller a fall. The quote should include:

- the contract length (time);
- date of start of contract;
- the forward rate for that period;
- the bid/offer spread.

The quote will take the form of a fixed interest rate for the identified period and a contract will be agreed according to commonly accepted terms. In the United Kingdom these are the ground rules established by the British Bankers Association and are universally known as the FRABBA terms. The quote will specify terms of settlement and a method of calculation of the amount due on settlement. The parties then exchange confirmations. The contract will detail:

- the period;
- the notional principal;
- the agreed rate;
- the market rate, used as a reference point for settlement.

On settlement date the contract is fulfilled by a single payment changing hands. The amount of this is arrived at by using the agreed settlement formula.

In *The Financial Jungle* Phil Rivett and Peter Speak of Coopers & Lybrand outline how a typical FRA works:

> Forward rates can be determined arithmetically by applying the interest rate differential ruling between the two currencies in question to the spot rate. The process of arbitrage will ensure that the linkage between interest and exchange rates is maintained. If the rates were not linked it would be possible to borrow money in one currency, convert it and deposit it in a different currency and cover the foreign currency exposure with a forward contract and make substantial profits. The process of arbitrage keeps the rates in line such that any potentially large profits are rapidly eliminated. Forward rates can therefore be calculated from the prevailing interest rates. For example:

US dollar interest rate	$6\frac{3}{4}\%$
Sterling interest rate	$1\frac{1}{4}\%$
Spot exchange rate	1.95

If £1m is borrowed for one year and immediately converted into $1.95m and deposited for one year the forward exchange rate for one year forward can be found by equating the two amounts as follows:

$$\frac{1.95 \times 1.0675}{1 \times 1.1125} = 1.8711$$

At this rate the maturing deposit of $2.08m could be converted to give £1.1125m to repay the loan and no arbitrage profit will arise.

The majority of interbank transactions in the forward market are foreign exchange swaps. A foreign exchange swap is the simultaneous purchase and sale of a given currency at two different dates. Usually a swap will combine a purchase or sale in the spot market with a forward transaction. The swap rate or swap price is the differential between the rates quoted for the two dates of the swap. Where one leg is a spot transaction, the spot price is equivalent to the forward premium or discount.

This computation is of course a very simple one. FRAs become much more complicated. In practice the writer will want to turn a profit and will offer a worse return for the buyer than the simple quote suggests.

The factors which influence the quote are:

- the bank's exposure to interest rate movements;
- credit standing/existing business record with the customer;
- availability of balance sheet reserves to cover the proposed deal.

FRAs become much more complicated

SWAPS

Currency and interest rate swaps

In an interest rate swap, no exchange of principal takes place but interest payments are made on the notional principal amount. In a currency swap the principal sum is usually exchanged:

- at the start;
- at the end;
- at a combination of both; or
- neither.

Swaps are infinitely flexible. In technical terms they are a method of exchanging the underlying economic basis of a debt or asset without affecting the underlying principal obligation on the debt or asset. Interest payments can be exchanged between two parties to achieve changes in the calculation of interest on the principal, for example:

A swap is a way of exchanging the underlying economic basis of an asset or debt without affecting the underlying principal obligation on it.

- floating to fixed;
- fixed to floating;
- LIBOR to prime based;
- prime to LIBOR;
- currency A to currency B.

In an interest rate swap both parties raise finance as they normally would in the markets where they have relative advantage. They then engage in the swap (Example 1.1 in chapter 1 illustrates one way in which this is done). The arrangement bene-

Swaps are infinitely flexible

fits both parties since it exploits one's comparative advantage: in Example 1.1 P is able to raise funds more cheaply than Q in both the fixed- and floating-rate markets but it has a greater advantage in the former – the market it does not wish to use.

Swaps of the type shown in Example 1.1 are known as 'plain vanilla' interest rate swaps and are used to alter the interest rate profile of assets or liabilities. This term can also be applied to simple currency swaps to alter the currency profile of assets or liabilities.

Many swaps are linked to the issue of a Eurobond (as in Example 1.1). An issuer offers a bond in a currency and instrument where it has the greatest competitive advantage. It then asks the underwriter of the bond to provide it with a swap to convert funds into the required type.

Other types of swaps

Basis rate swaps

These are broadly similar to plain vanilla swaps but in a basis rate swap both legs are floating rate but measured against different benchmarks.

Asset swaps

These can be either a plain vanilla or a basis rate swap. Instead of swapping the interest payments on liability, one of the parties to the swap is swapping the interest receipts on an asset.

Currency swaps

These involve an exchange of liabilities between currencies. A currency swap can consist of three stages:

- A spot exchange of principal – this forms part of the swap agreement as a similar effect can be obtained by using the spot foreign exchange market.

- Continuing exchange of interest payments during the term of the swap – this represents a series of forward foreign exchange contracts during the term of the swap contract. The contract is typically fixed at the same exchange rate as the spot rate used at the outset of the swap.
- Re-exchange of principal on maturity.

A currency swap has the following benefits:

- Treasurers can hedge currency risk.
- It can provide considerable cost savings. So a strong borrower in the Deutschmark market may get a better US dollar rate by raising funds in the Deutschmark market and swapping them for US dollars.
- The swap market permits funds to be accessed in currencies which may otherwise command a high premium.
- It offers diversification of borrowings.

A more complex version of a currency swap is a currency coupon swap, which swaps a fixed- or floating-rate interest payment in one currency for a floating-rate payment in another. These are also known as circus swaps.

Non-generic swaps

Any non-plain vanilla or currency swaps are called non-generic swaps. New types of swap are being invented regularly. The following are among them.

Mortgage swaps

> ***New types of swap are being invented regularly***

A mortgage swap seeks to emulate the economic process of buying a collection of mortgage-backed securities and financing the acquisition with short-term variable-rate debt. It has been described as an interest rate swap with a long-term forward commitment. Three factors distinguish a mortgage swap from an interest rate swap:

- a reducing principal amount;
- periodic cash settlements for adjustments to the premium or discount resulting from prepayment;
- settlement with cash or delivery of securities at a prearranged date.

Amortising swaps

These are swaps for which the notional principal falls over its term. They are particularly useful for borrowers who have issued redeemable debt. It enables them to match interest rate hedging with the redemption profile of the bonds.

Forward swaps

These are swaps arranged to run from some point in the future. They are similar to FRAs but are longer-term vehicles.

Swaptions

Options on swaps, they give the buyer of the swaption the right but not the obligation to enter into a swap agreement where term, notional principal and interest rates are predetermined. They are helpful in tenders where the bidder needs to fix costs but does not know who will win the contract.

Callable swaps

There are similar to swaptions but here the swap counterparty has the right to end the swap.

Canapé swaps

These currency swaps have no initial or final exchange of principal. Interest payments in one currency are exchanged for interest payments in another.

The price of a swap

The price of swaps is determined by several factors, dictated by commercial supply and demand, particularly interest and currency rate swaps. A swap trader, when fixing a price, will take into account his or her bid/offer spread, which is itself influenced by a range of factors including the trader's existing position and the creditworthiness of the client. In the US dollar market it is normal practice to quote swaps as a margin over US Treasury bonds. The fixed leg of the swap is stated as a number of points over the Treasury rate for bonds of the same maturity as the swap. By convention the floating leg features as six-month US$ LIBOR.

Hedging with swaps

Swaps are used for two main functions: trading and hedging. In hedging their functions cover many situations, among which are:

- hedging new or existing debt or assets by switching floating-rate borrowings to fixed rate and vice versa;
- matching exposure to foreign currencies;
- with currency swaps, matching positions where borrowings are denominated in one currency and assets in another.

Position taking

Swaps can also be used to create an overall interest rate or currency position. This could be termed 'structural hedging' and is done in three ways:

- the basic matched swap;
- the basic hedged swap;
- portfolio hedging.

The basic matched swap involves matching each swap transaction with an equal and opposite swap transaction. The terms of the matching swap are identical. The bank takes a fee. It charges 10 basis points (that is, 0.1 per cent) on the contract for assuming the credit risk on each counterparty. The credit risk apart, this technique enjoys relatively low overall risk. The downside is that it is severely limited in flexibility and it hinges on locating an equal and opposite counterparty in the market. For all practical purposes, banks may consider the swap to be matched if key elements are similar but not identical.

The basic hedged swap was created in response to the demand for greater flexibility and is handy in the US$ swap market, where hedges are simple to put together. It allows a bank to create a swap for one customer and then hold the swap in a warehouse until a suitable counterparty emerges. An inherent risk in this solution is that by the time suitable counterparties have been found interest rates will have moved, locking in a loss. This risk is then hedged in a synthetic swap (see Glossary).

Portfolio hedging amalgamates all cash flows in the total swaps book and aims to hedge the net position. The net position is hedged using other swaps, FRAs, futures, options or bonds. The US$ swap market favours this approach because it offers:

- ability to hedge;
- flexibility in structuring swaps;
- efficiency in hedging only the net position;
- a reduction in reinvestment risk through the netting of surpluses and deficits.

On the downside, however:

- complex analysis is needed to fashion the optimal hedge;
- the approach is prone to loss of information about individual deals
- monitoring hedges takes up a great deal of time.

FUTURES CONTRACTS

Financial futures comprise three principal types:

- interest rate futures;
- currency futures;
- stock index futures.

Interest rate futures centre on specific types of financial instruments, whose prices are dependent on interest rates. Currency futures are based on internationally significant currencies. Stock index futures draw on internationally recognised stock exchange indices.

Mechanics of a futures contract

A financial futures contract is purchased or sold through a broker. It is a commitment to make or take delivery of a specified financial instrument, or perform a particular service, at a predetermined date in the future (see Example 5.1). The price of the contract is established at the outset.

Holders of open futures contracts will see potential profits and losses fluctuate as the market price moves before delivery date. The standardised format of futures contract makes such gains and losses easy to monitor. Price movements are followed and recorded as minimum price variations – known as ticks – and carry a defined value for each contract type.

A financial futures contract is a commitment to make or take delivery of a specified financial instrument at a predetermined future date.

Example 5.1

Buying a June three-month LIFFE Eurodollar contract commits the purchaser to make a deposit of 1,000,000 Eurodollars in June for three months at an agreed interest rate implicit in the price. Similarly, the sale of a June three-month Eurodollar contract commits the vendor to take a deposit of 1,000,000 Eurodollars in June for three months at an agreed interest rate. These commitments may be set off against each other.

The price of a Eurodollar contract is quoted on an index basis, that is, 100 minus the annual interest rate on a three-month time deposit. Each tick represents $25, being three months' interest on $1 million at a rate of 0.01 per cent. An increase in the index from 85.05 to 85.10 is a change of five ticks, or $125 per contract. So someone who has bought ten such contracts at 85.05 will potentially realise a gain of $1,250 (10 × 5 × $25). This is the same as the profit that would be made by taking a £10 million deposit for three months at 14.90 per cent and making a similar deposit at 14.95 per cent. To realise the gain, he or she could sell ten contracts at the current market price of 85.10.

A futures contract is executed by depositing an agreed 'initial margin' with a futures broker. At the end of each trading day, any changes in market value are charged or credited to customers' accounts based on this mark to market. Such changes are referred to as the variation margin. If this rises above the initial margin the customer may withdraw the excess. If the account falls below the maintenance margin – slightly less than the initial margin – then a margin call is made and the customer is required to supply funds.

The distinction between the maintenance margin and initial margin is decided by individual exchanges. Factors include:

- type of contract;
- face value of the contract;

- historical volatility of prices;
- whether the contract is intended as a hedge or is speculative.

As with swaps, financial futures have two main functions: trading and hedging. The aim of trading futures is to benefit from price rises or falls in underlying instruments without having to buy those instruments. Trading is therefore speculative. It reflects a willingness to take a risk, based on a view on the way interest or currency rates will move in the markets, in order to make a profit.

Some traders hold open positions on futures contracts to enable them to respond to changing market conditions with a high degree of flexibility. Some may be interested in exploiting minute-by-minute gains – or scalping as the technique is known. Others will hold their positions open for many months while waiting for long-term trends to have an impact on the markets. They may take a view on relative movements in prices between different delivery dates on the same contracts (straddle trading) or a cross-contract (spread trading). A further distinct type of operation undertaken by traders is arbitrage, i.e. taking advantage of movements in the markets for profit-taking purposes.

Example 5.2 shows a futures transactions and Example 5.3 a hedge using futures.

Example 5.2

On 1 October a dealer predicts that interest rates will fall towards the end of the year. The current rate for three-month deposits is 15 per cent. He aims to make a profit from his opinion that rates will decline. So he buys four December three-month sterling interest rate futures at the current rate of 85.00.

The early December rate for the contract is 86.50, or an interest rate of 13.5 per cent. So he closes down his position. The transactions would follow this pattern:

Cash flows	£
1 October Buy four December three-month sterling interest rate contracts (at £500,000 each) at 85.00	
Initial margin paid (4 × £1,000)	(4,000.00)
Prior to early December Three-month sterling interest rate contracts gradually rise and then stabilise as interest rates fall	
Variation margin received: 150 ticks (86.50 – 85.00) × 4 × £12.50 per tick	7,500.00
Early December Sell futures contract resulting in return of initial margin	4,000.00
Profit	7,500.00

Example 5.3

A corporate treasurer has borrowings of $80 million in Eurodollars with a six-month rollover next due on 1 December. In October he decides that interest rates are going to rise from the current 10.5 per cent. The price of December three-month Eurodollar interest rate contracts is 89.00, reflecting a yield of 11 per cent. He is convinced that rates will go above this.

The aim is to hedge against interest rate costs until the time of the next rollover. So he sells 160 December three-month Eurodollar interest rate contracts. Double the capital value is needed to lock in the rate for six months. So 2 × 80 – or 160 – contracts are required. On 1 December the price of contracts is 85.75 (14.25 per cent yield) and the interest rate on the rollover was 14 per cent. He closes out his position.

A comparison between the futures market and the cash markets in Example 5.3 reveals that the futures contract wins hands down. The cost of borrowing on the cash market was $11.2 million, whereas operating a futures contract raised $1.3 million profit as well as offering the protection required.

Learning points

1 Derivatives are classified as forwards-based or options-based contracts.

2 Forwards-based products are grouped into three types:
(a) forward contract;
(b) swaps;
(c) futures contract.

3 In the main, forwards are simpler and more conventional products than options. Some foreign exchange and forwards-based products have been available since the earliest days of futures contracts.

4 A forward contract is the simplest derivative. Large numbers of them are traded every day. Two parties – buyer and seller – sign a contract for a product or service at some date in the future at a specified price. The price of the contract is tied to a nominated underlying.

5 A swap is a contract to exchange cash flows – usually one fixed and one floating rate. They can normally be classified as interest rate, currency, commodity and equity.

6 Swaps vary in complexity. The most commonly used swap is the plain vanilla interest rate swap – the basic model.

7 The futures contract is an exchange-traded contract which is usually smaller in size and value than a forward or swap.

6

OPTIONS-BASED DERIVATIVES

SUMMARY

This chapter is an examination of options-based products. It describes the objectives of options products, how they operate and how they create value for clients.

- **what options are – the right, not the obligation, to buy or sell**
- **how options work – and how the value is calculated**
- **the key attributes of options – calls and puts**
- **the various classifications of options-based derivatives**
- **profit and loss characteristics of options**
- **exchange-traded options**
- **caps, floors and collars**

‘Options are different from all other financial instruments’

‘The main purposes of options are trading and hedging’

‘OTC options are . . . either American or European products’

THE FUNCTIONS OF OPTIONS

The second of the two principal building blocks in derivatives is options. These products offer, in exchange for a premium, the right – but *not* the obligation – to buy or sell the underlying at the strike price during a period or on a specific date. So the owner of the option can choose not to exercise the option and let it expire. A buyer can benefit from favourable movements in the price of the underlying but is not exposed to corresponding losses. This represents the principal difference between forwards and options.

It is summarised neatly by JP Morgan and Arthur Andersen's *Guide to Corporate Exposure Management* (appearing in *Risk Magazine*): 'The advantage of options over swaps and forwards is that options give the buyer the desired protection while allowing him to benefit from a favourable movement in the underlying price.'

Privately negotiated options exist on a multitude of underlyings such as bonds, equities, currencies and commodities, and even swaps. Options can also be structured as securities in warrants or can be embedded in products like convertible bonds, certain commodity- or equity-linked bonds with options.

PRICING OPTIONS

Phil Rivett and Peter Speak say in *The Financial Jungle*:

> The overall price of an option is the sum of its intrinsic value and its time value.
>
> *Intrinsic value*
> The intrinsic value of an option is the benefit to the holder if he were to exercise the option immediately. At the time of expiry of the option the value of the option is its intrinsic value and will be determined from a comparison of the difference between the

market value of the underlying transaction and the exercise price of the option. For in the money options, the intrinsic value of the option is the difference between the market value of the underlying transaction and the strike price of the option.

For a call option, this can be shown as follows [see figure 6.1].

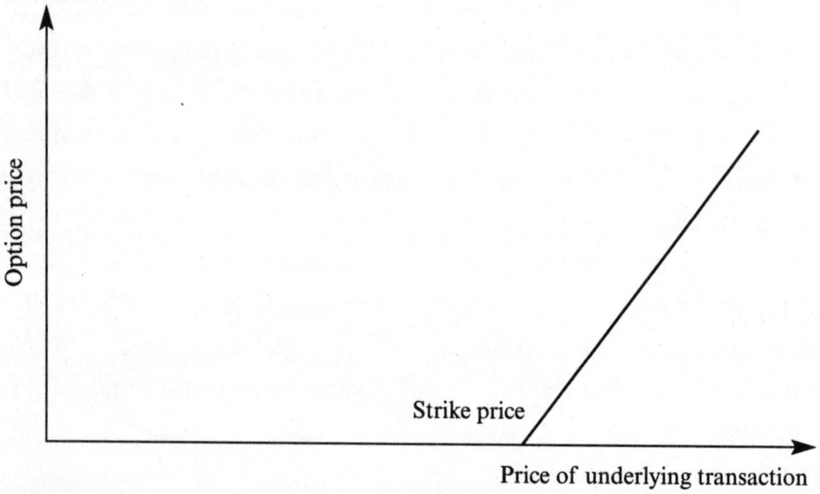

Figure 6.1 The intrinsic value of an option at expiry

Source: *The Financial Jungle*

For at the money or out of the money options the intrinsic value is nil. The intrinsic value of an option can never be less than nil. For example, when the market price is below the strike price a call option will not be exercised and the owner of such an option will obtain no benefit.

Time value

The time value is the difference between the market value of the option and its intrinsic value. For an in the money call option, the time value can be calculated as follows:

Call option time value = option price + strike price
– price of underlying transaction.

For example, if the market value of ICI ordinary shares is 360p, and the market value of the ICI January 350p call option on the London Traded Options Market is 30p, the time value is 20p (30 + 350 – 360). Alternatively, the time value can be described as the call option price (30p) less the intrinsic value of 10p (360 – 350). For an out of the money option, the time value represents the whole of the value of the option premium as the intrinsic value is nil. Amongst the factors which determine the time value of an option are:

- The proximity of the market value of the underlying transaction to the strike price of the option. At any time an option will have the greatest time value if the price of the underlying transaction is equal to the strike price of the option and it will decrease if the option moves either deeply in to or out of the money. This is illustrated in the following diagram of the time value of a call option for a range of different values of the underlying transaction [see figure 6.2].

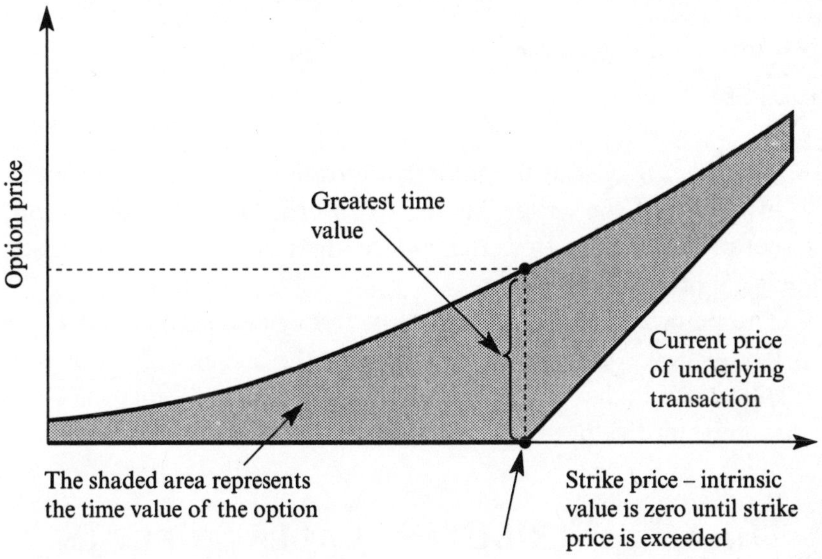

Figure 6.2 The time value of option

Source: *The Financial Jungle*

- The remaining life to expiry – the time value of an option will decrease over its life as the risk of the writer of the option diminishes. At expiry, the time value will be nil. The rate of decay of the time value increases the closer the option comes to expiry, as can be seen in the following diagram [see figure 6.3].

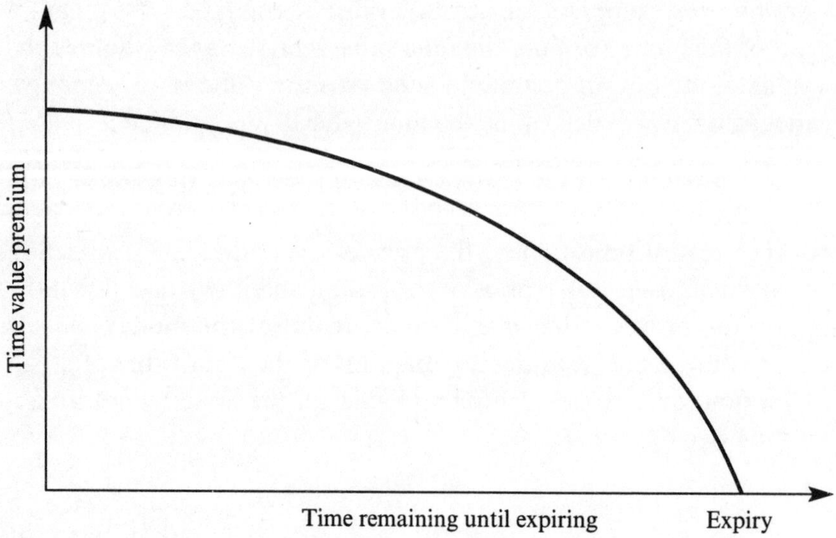

Figure 6.3 The rate of decay of the time value of an option

Source: *The Financial Jungle*

- The holding cost of the underlying transaction – the amount of interest that the writer has to pay in order to cover the option, net of any receipts from the underlying transaction (eg dividends or coupons).
- The perceived future volatility of the prices of the underlying transaction – the greater the volatility, the higher will be the premium demanded by the writer of the option to compensate for the greater risk of unfavourable price movements.

THE KEY ATTRIBUTES – CALLS AND PUTS

An option is a contract which has one or other of two key attributes – to buy (call) or to sell (put). The purchaser is called the buyer or holder, the seller is called the writer or grantor. The premium may be expressed as a percentage of the price per unit of the underlying.

The holder of an American option has the right to exercise the contract at any stage during the period of the option,

A call option confers on the holder the right (but not the obligation) to buy the underlying contract or instrument at a fixed price during or at the end of the option period, as the case may be.

Conversely, a put option confers on the holder the right (but not the obligation) to sell the underlying at a fixed price.

whereas the holder of a European option can exercise his right only at the end of the period.

During or at the end of the contract period (depending on the 'nationality' of the option), the holder can do as he pleases. He can buy or sell (as the case may be) the underlying, let the contract expire or sell the option contract itself in the market.

PROFIT AND LOSS CHARACTERISTICS OF OPTIONS

Options are different from all other financial instruments. The attribute of right without obligation sets them apart from the other risk-management tools. They have one-sided risk and return. Option writers' profits are limited to the premiums they receive but potential losses can be unlimited.

Options . . . have one-sided risk and return

The profit and loss implications of two options positions are indicated in figures 6.4 and 6.5, which show the relationship to profit of a position if held through to expiry. Figure 6.4 shows the profit characteristics for a buyer of a call option. It has the added advantage of providing insurance against any downward movement in the price of security.

The maximum loss is the premium paid and this is fixed for any price of the underlying below the exercise price. As price moves above the exercise price the potential for profit is unlimited.

Conversely, figure 6.5 shows the position when selling a call

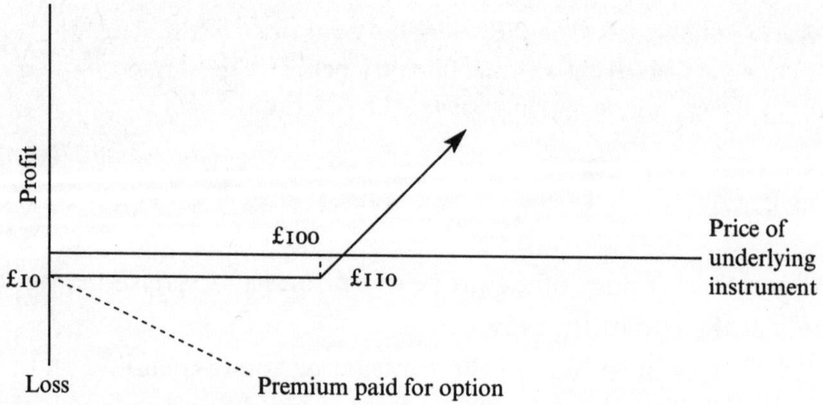

Figure 6.4 Buy a call option

option. When the underlying falls below the strike price, the maximum that can be made is the premium received. If the price of the underlying rises above the strike price, the probability of the option being exercised against the writer increases and the loss potential is infinite.

For a written put, on the other hand, if the price of the underlying is more than the strike price, the option would not be exercised – because the holder would be better off selling the underlying in the market. If the option is not exercised, the writer's gain is restricted to the premium received. If the price of

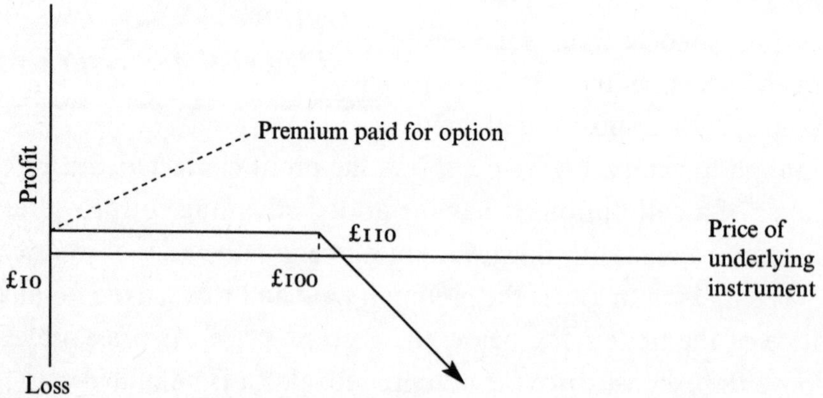

Figure 6.5 Sell a call option

the underlying drops below the strike price and the option is exercised, the writer's loss will come to the strike price paid to the holder minus the value of the underlying less the value of the premium. The potential loss is thus the price of the underlying less the premium received, and the maximum loss would be incurred if the underlying became worthless.

In practice an option will always have a positive time value

The diagrams suffer from being somewhat simplistic and they refer only to the expiry. During its life, in practice an option will always have a positive time value. So an option's time value will tend to smooth out the trends.

As with forwards, the main purposes of options are trading and hedging. The four 'naked' or uncovered positions – buy a call, write a call, buy a put, write a put – have already been discussed. Hedges, spreads and combinations are types of covered positions where one or more securities protect the position of other securities, all related to the same underlying stock

HEDGING

Hedging is especially attractive because it provides a defence against unfavourable changes in rate and at the same time affords the opportunity to benefit from favourable changes. Contingent cash flows can also be hedged. An option combines with an underlying to protect either the option or the underlying. Such hedges include:

- long in the underlying with a written position in calls or a purchased position in puts;
- short in the underlying with a purchased position in calls or a written position in puts.

Hedging is especially attractive

Such option strategies are extremely powerful. If faced with an exposure, three choices are available: (a) cover forward, (b) deal with the exposure when it arises (wait and see) and (c) use options. A typical example of using options is to manage risk on currency exposure. In the long run the economic policies of (a) and (b) should be consistent except for a time lag. This would arise because the forward rate at any one time is a function of the current spot rate plus an interest differential.

The overall objective of the hedge is to smooth out returns, guarantee a minimum return or ensure a guaranteed level of return when taking advantage of speculative and beneficial movements. Example 6.1 illustrates hedging using options.

Example 6.1

A Swiss company hopes to win a construction contract in the United States. The company is in a dilemma because it does not want a futures or forward position to sell profits forward since it is possible that the company will not secure the contract. An outright position in US dollars might result in large losses if the US dollar decreased in value against the Swiss franc.

The company takes a put option as it wants to be able to sell dollars at a fixed price. It fears that the dollar will fall and it needs insurance against this happening. The business locks in profits with a price fixed in dollar terms

Covered calling

The most popular strategy is described as covered call writing and involves writing one call against each share owned of the underlying stock. The relevant figures for a purchased stock and a written call are shown in figure 6.6. The profit–loss line for the combined position is determined, for each value of the underlying instrument at expiry, by adding together the vertical distances of the two separate profit–loss lines from the horizontal axes.

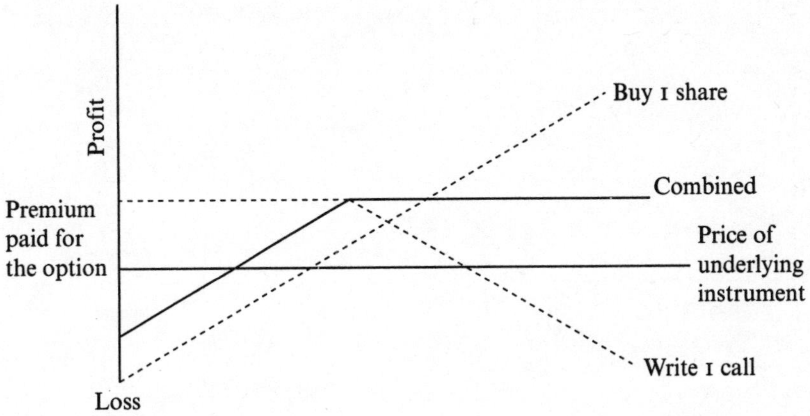

Figure 6.6 Covered call writing

Whether or not an option will be exercised will depend on the circumstances:

- if the option price exceeds the spot price:
  - the holder will exercise a put;
  - the holder will not exercise a call;
- if the spot price exceeds the option price:
  - the holder will exercise a call;
  - the holder will not exercise a put.

SPREADS AND COMBINATIONS

A spread combines put or call options on the same underlying instrument but with different expiration dates or strike prices, where some are bought and others are written. Three common spreads are the bull spread, bear spread and butterfly spread. The operation and profit profile of each are described below.

Bull spread

Operation The option purchased has the lower strike price (see figure 6.7).

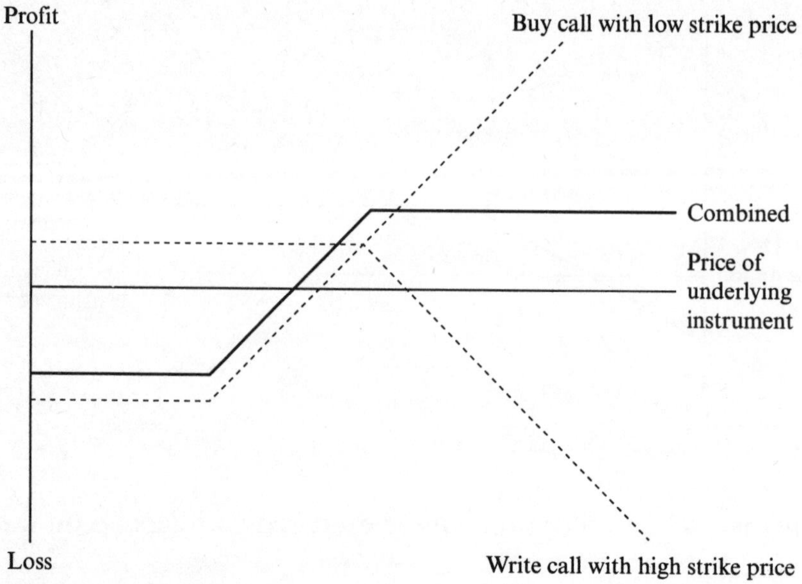

Figure 6.7 Bull spread

Two simple forms of this strategy are possible:

- buy a call and sell another call at a higher strike price;
- buy a put and sell another put at a higher strike price.

Profit profile Profits and losses are limited to a maximum of the purchase price of the options. The reduced probability of gain is balanced by the reduced probability of loss.

When to use If you believe the market will rise but have reservations and wish to protect your position.

Bear spread

Operation The option purchased has the higher strike price (see figure 6.8). Two simple forms of this strategy are possible:

- sell a call and buy another call at a higher strike price;
- sell a put and buy another put at a higher strike price.

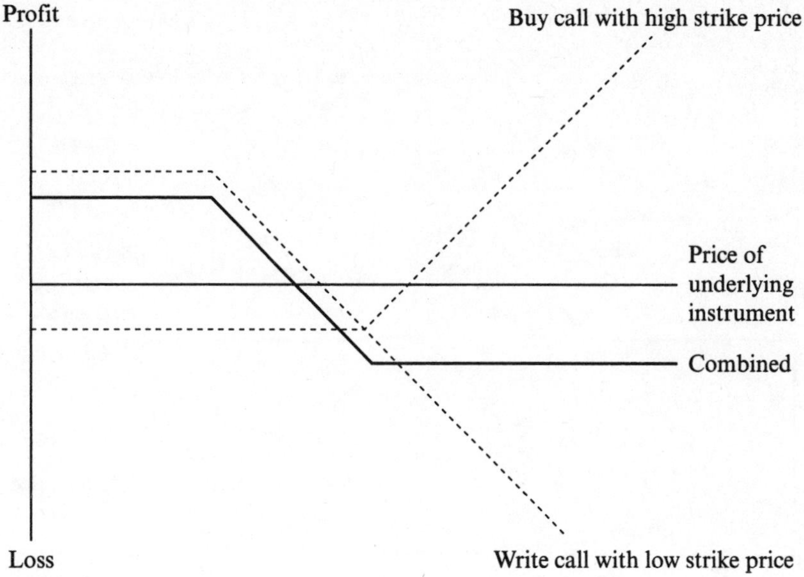

Figure 6.8 Bear spread

Profit profile As for a bull spread, the profit and loss are limited to the purchase price of the options.

When to use If you believe the market is more likely to fall than rise but at the same time you wish to protect your position.

Butterfly spread

Operation Two options in the middle, with respect to strike price, are written against buying one option on each side, all on the same underlying instrument. Figure 6.9 illustrates the strategy, which is as follows:

- buy a call at E1 (i.e. strike price is E1);
- sell two calls at E2;
- buy a call at E3.

Profit profile The maximum profit occurs when the market price of the underlying instrument stays near the strike price of

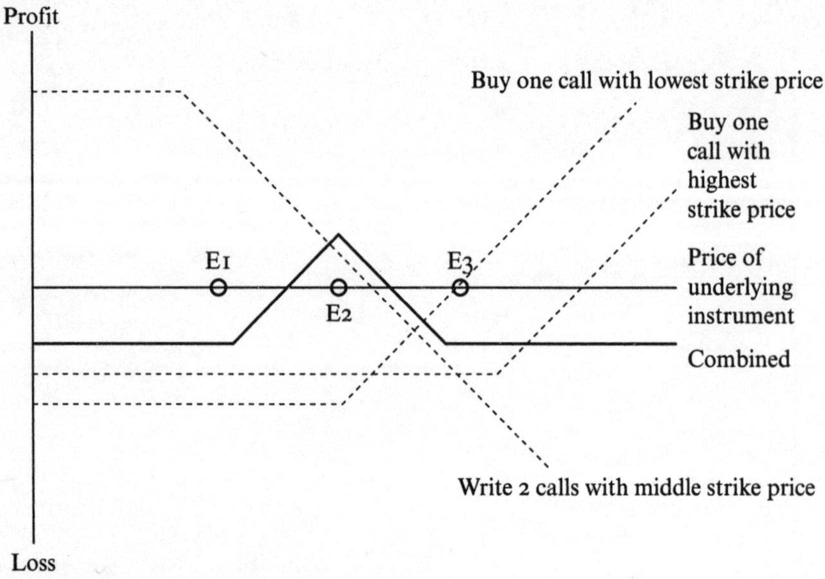

Figure 6.9 Butterfly spread

the written calls (at E2) while the maximum loss is the cost of purchasing the options.

When to use This is the most advantageous in a stable market when the strike price is between E1 and E2. It is a conservative strategy.

Combination

A combination strategy combines puts and calls on the same underlying instrument so that they are either bought or both written. The most popular combinations are straddles and strangles, which are described below.

Short straddle

Operation Sell a put and a call at the same exercise price (see figure 6.10).

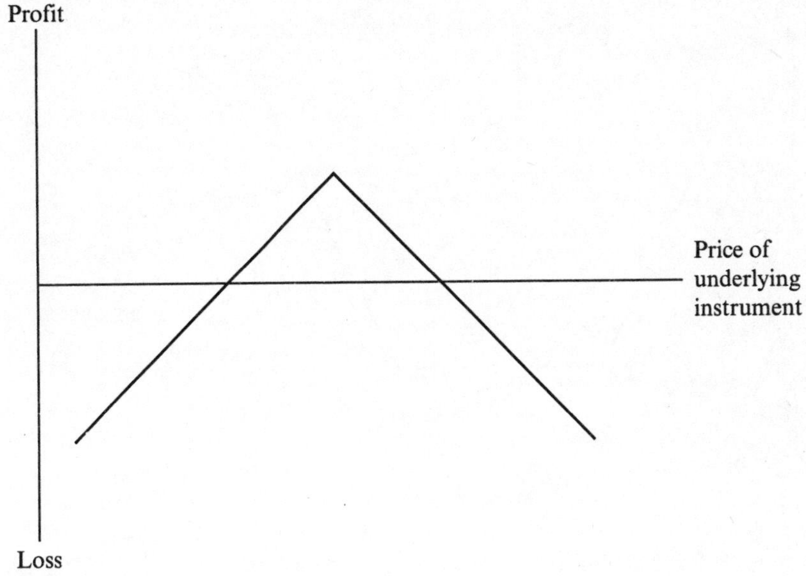

Figure 6.10 Short straddle

Profit profile The profit is limited to the selling price of the options. The maximum profit is obtained if the price of the underlying instrument remains near the common strike price (i.e. experiences low volatility), and the loss potential is open-ended.

When to use If you believe that the price of the underlying instrument is to remain approximately constant. This is a speculative strategy.

Long strangle

Operation This is similar to a straddle except that the puts and calls are bought at different prices (see figure 6.11).

Profit profile This is similar to a straddle but the maximum loss is smaller and there have to be larger fluctuations in the underlying instrument to enable profits to be made.

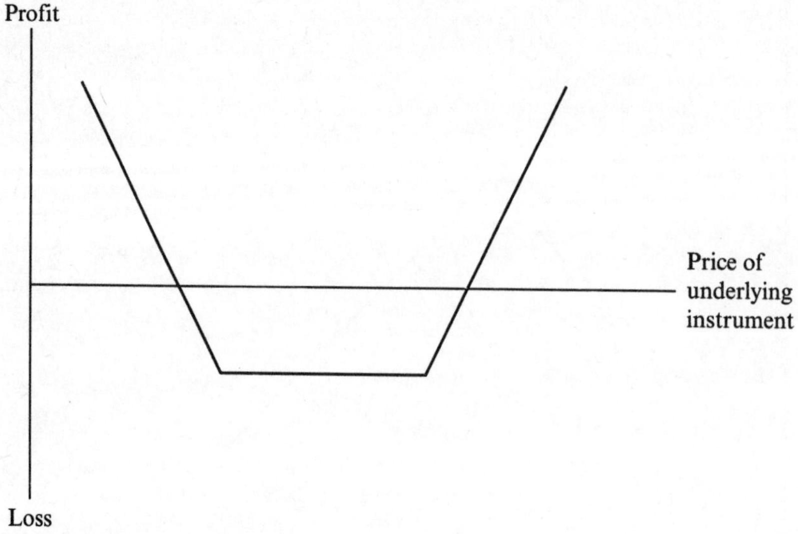

Figure 6.11 Long strangle

When to use When you expect there to be very large fluctuations in the market.

These profit/loss figures provide a good way to become familiar with various trading strategies. However, to interpret them correctly it is important to remember their limitations. They are valid only if all parts of the position are held until expiration.

Since many involve selling as well as buying options, it is not a certainty that they would be held until expiration unless the options can be exercised only at that time, as in a European option.

THE BEHAVIOUR OF OPTIONS

Several models exist for working out the price of options contracts. Generally they relate the option price to the following factors:

- market conditions;
- spot price;
- strike price;
- time to expiry;
- the volatility of the price of the underlying;
- the level of interest rates.

General market conditions

The following factors can lead to an improvement in the option premium:

- imposition of exchange controls;
- imposition of withholding taxes;
- illiquidity in spot or forward markets.

An increased premium would reflect an additional risk to the writer in a deal in which one or both currencies were subject to the conditions above.

Other factors

Value is determined by the following factors:

- the exercise period – the longer it is, the greater the probability that the contract will be worth something;
- volatility – is a measure of the status of the underlying: the larger the volatility, the more likely it is that a profit will be made from the option;
- interest rates – these play a key role in determining the value of options. For calls, pushing up the interest rate decreases the present value of the exercise price and increases the value of the option. Puts are the opposite but for currency options the situation is more complex.

OTC OPTIONS

OTC options are designed to meet those specific demands of companies that may not be fully supplied by exchange-traded options. OTC options are used by end-users mainly for hedging purposes since exposure can be individually offset. OTC products are used to hedge exposure in the foreign exchange markets and to limit interest rate exposures not only in different instruments but also in different markets.

OTC options are structured as either American or European products. In Europe the units are quoted in a domestic currency and must be changed into the dollar equivalent using the spot rate. The US dollar equivalent then becomes the historical cost basis against which future mark to market is totalled. OTC options are also written against short-term interest rate securities.

OTC options are not listed on exchanges so the closing prices may be calculated using one of the four main option-pricing models: Black–Scholes, Cox Rubenstein, Leland and Garman–Kohlhagen. They share the key factors which determine pricing:

- current asset price;
- exercise price;
- time to expiry;
- volatility;
- risk-free interest rates;
- exchange rates where relevant.

STANDARD OPTION TECHNIQUES TO ACHIEVE PARTICULAR RESULTS

Interest rate caps, floors and collars

An interest rate cap is an agreement by the seller to pay the buyer the excess of the prevailing market index over a 'cap' rate based on the agreed notional principal amount. The prevailing market index is normally a short-term rate such as LIBOR, commercial paper or Treasury bills.

A cap agreement provides the buyer with interest rate protection similar to a series of European put options on the same index. Caps provide much greater flexibility than options because they are individually tailored.

A floor is the reverse of a cap. It is an agreement by the floor seller to pay the buyer an excess of an agreed minimum rate. A collar is a combination of a purchased cap and a written floor. The most common type of option used with floors and caps is the average price option. This is also known as the Asian option. Here the strike price is compared with the settlement price – based on the average of prices prevailing over a defined period – to assess whether and by how much the option is in the money at expiry.

According to JP Morgan, average price options are popular for two key reasons:

- They are a superior hedge for businesses which trade continually. This is because they match actual commodity expenditure more often than options struck at the price prevailing at a single time.
- They cost less than standard options. This is because the average price over a month is less volatile than the daily price. Option premiums are higher when the price of the underlying is more volatile.

OPTIONS MARKETS

In *The Financial Jungle* the following European options markets are listed (cross-references appearing in the original have been omitted):

- *The London Traded Options Market* (LTOM) was established in 1978 as part of the International Stock Exchange. The options are for UK publicly listed equities and options on the FT-SE 100 index. The contract size for equities is usually for 1,000 shares and contracts are traded by open outcry. Premiums must be paid on the day following the trade and all bargains except for currency options are registered and settled at the London Options Clearing House Limited (LOCH). LTOM is in the process of merging with LIFFE. [*Author's note:* the merger has now taken place, but full integration is still in progress.]
- *Foreign currency OTC options* in the interbank market in London are usually traded on BBA terms for the London Interbank Currency Option Market (LICOM). When granted, a LICOM option can be designated as European or American.
- *The European Options Exchange* (EOE) in Amsterdam. The EOE has traded options on equities, currencies, government bonds, bond and stock indices and bullion. The trading cycle is quarterly with options for the closest two months available for currency options in Dutch guilders against sterling and the US dollar. All bargains are cleared through the European Option Clearing Corporation (EOCC) which is owned by the EOE and which guarantees the commitments and monitors the margin requirements of the EOE.
- *Swiss Options and Financial Futures Exchange* (SOFFEX). In May 1988 SOFFEX, a fully integrated electronic trading and clearing system for options, commenced operations in Switzerland. SOFFEX trades options on the Swiss market index as well as a number of equities of major Swiss companies. The standard size of a contract is for five shares (due to the high price of most Swiss shares). The options are American with a maximum life of six months. There are standard expiry dates with an option expiring on the Saturday after the third Friday in any of the three months following the month of creation of the option.
- *Deutsche Terminbörse* (DTB). In Germany options on major German and foreign stocks and options on German government bonds are traded on the Frankfurt and Düsseldorf stock exchanges, although the volume is low. In 1990 the DTB commenced trading equity options in a standard size of 50 shares.

- *The Stockholm Options Market* (SOM) was established in 1985. The SOM offers options on Swedish and Norwegian shares, on an equity index (OMX) and currency options and futures denominated in deutschmarks and Swedish kroner, both against the US dollar. The 55 members of the SOM execute transactions on an electronic system which automatically clears the trades. The SOM has grown substantially with the OMX being one of the most liquid European stock index options. The SOM is owned by Swedish banks and futures and options brokers and its shares are listed on the Stockholm Stock Exchange. OM London, a wholly owned subsidiary of SOM, also trades the OMX option contract. A real time computer link with SOM means that the two exchanges (London and Stockholm) operate as a single marketplace with the contract having the same liquidity in each. OM London also trades Swedish and Norwegian equity options.

- In France options on interest rates, white sugar and deutschmarks are traded on the MATIF. In addition the *Marché des Options Négociables de la Bourse de Paris* (MONEP) trades options on French equities (usually in 100 share lots) as well as the CAC 40 index.

- There are also option exchanges in Copenhagen (*Guarantee Fund for Danish Options and Futures*) with contracts in mortgage bonds, government bonds, a stock index as well as options on Danish equities. In Helsinki the *Finnish Options Brokers* exchange has equity options and an index option.

Learning points

1. Options are contracts which give the holder the right *but not the obligation* to buy or sell a specified commodity at a specified date in the future.

2. Option approaches are either call (buy) or put (sell).

3. The value of an option is determined by two factors: its intrinsic value (payoff at valuation) plus the time element.

4 Value is influenced by two factors: the duration of the contract and the volatility of the underlying.

5 Standard types of options are caps, floors and collars. Caps put an upper limit on aspects of the contract, whereas floors set the minimum level of exposure. Collars do both.

6 Spreads – bull, bear and butterfly – are strategies for trading in options.

7

DERIVATIVES SOLUTIONS AT WORK

SUMMARY

This chapter looks at various types of exposures and how they are handled with derivatives solutions:

- **general applications of derivatives to many business exposures**
- **basic building blocks using these solutions**
- **examples of derivatives at work**
- **interest rate exposures**
- **currency rate exposures**
- **commodity exposures**
- **equity exposures**

'Most derivatives are futures instruments'

'The key phrase . . . with options is: the right but not the obligation'

'Even domestic producers . . . are subjected to currency risk'

The notion that derivatives are an esoteric or exotic solution to risk-management issues has become a fallacy. In the corporate sector throughout the world their use for hedging a range of financial risk scenarios is now widespread. In recent years their application as instruments for meeting business risk has been expanded to back a range of products in the personal financial areas. A wide variety of new pensions, mortgages, insurance and other personal investment portfolio products have used derivatives. And, despite some horrendous losses, nine out of ten corporate users pronounced themselves satisfied with derivatives-backed products, according to a variety of market surveys.

In cases such as these derivatives can give enhanced stability to balance sheets and thus increase confidence in the business using derivatives products correctly. The growing flexibility offered by derivatives means that management can choose from an ever wider array of underlyings on which to base their risk-management approaches. And, although the complexities of derivatives are still not widely understood, some simple appreciation of their functioning is dawning in corporate treasuries and executive suites.

THE BASICS

We have already seen in the two previous chapters that derivatives are constructed from two building blocks:

- forwards-based products;
- options-based products.

All derivatives products and portfolios are constructed from these two units. In many cases they are built from a combination of a number of forwards or options, or both. Chapter 10 contains a full glossary of derivatives products and the categories into which they fall.

FORWARDS-BASED DERIVATIVES

Most derivatives are futures instruments. Forwards-based products allow buyers to purchase a transaction at some date in the future. Forwards become swaps when they extend into more than one time period. Figure 7.1 shows the extent of exposure when using a swap.

Using an example from *Risk Magazine*:

> a firm which borrows at LIBOR rate plus 80 base points has an underlying short position in LIBOR. That is the firm gains if LIBOR decreases and loses if LIBOR increases. A forward can be used as hedge – in this case buying the contract creates a long position in LIBOR. So the firm's borrowing is locked in at the forward rate plus 80 basis points. This is shown as the line coinciding with the horizontal axis. When LIBOR rises, gains on the swap or forward offset losses from the rises in rates; when LIBOR falls, losses on the contract are offset by gains on the underlying exposure. Thus the firm is insulated against changes in LIBOR, but at the price of forgoing the benefit of decreasing rates.

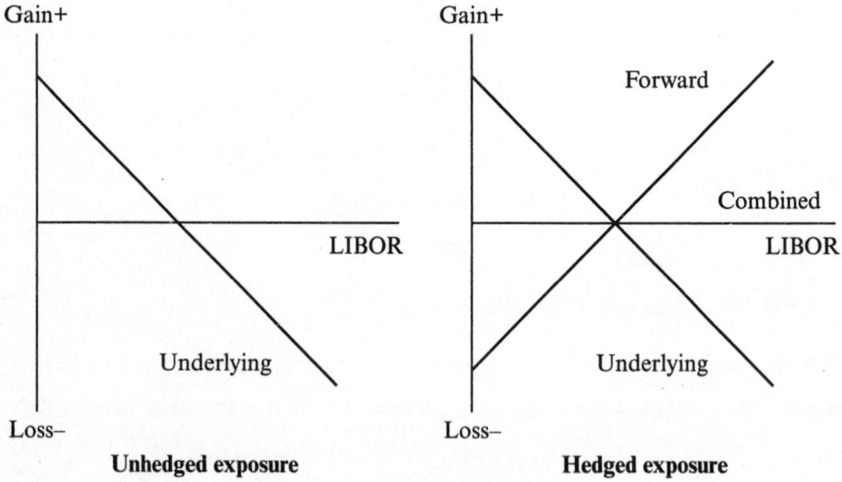

Figure 7.1 Hedging exposure by means of a swap

Source: *Risk Magazine*

OPTIONS

The key phrase to remember with options is: the right *but not the obligation* (in a transaction) to buy or sell at an agreed price at some specified date in the future. The option can take two forms: a call or a put. The call is an option to buy and the put an option to sell. A fee, or premium, is payable for the right and the contract must have a set expiry date.

Options can demonstrate advantages over forwards in that they give the desired protection while allowing the buyer to benefit from favourable changes in the price of the underlying.

Figure 7.2 indicates the exposure created by an option. This example is called the uncovered option. The figure shows the risk profiles of call options and put options. In the case of the call option, the purchaser buys, for 60 basis points (in a stipulated currency), a contract which has a strike price of 5.20 per cent. Until LIBOR rises to 5.20 per cent, the option is out of the money, that is, it pays nothing.

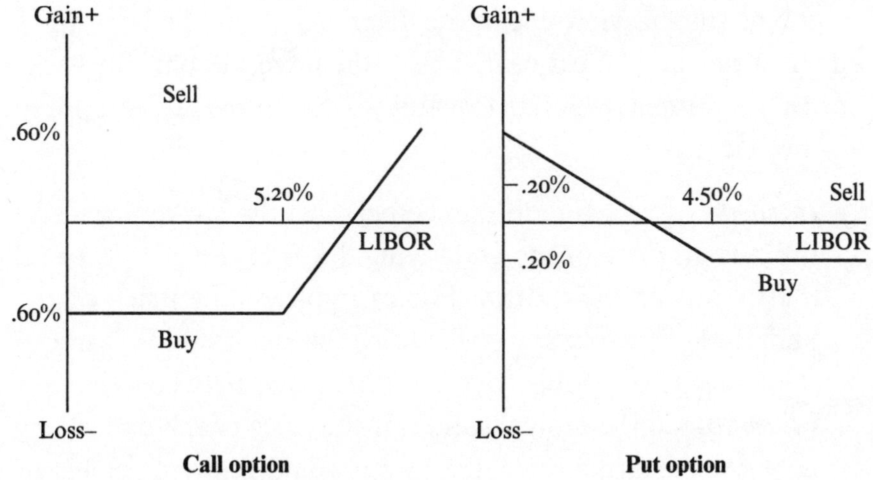

Figure 7.2 The exposure created by an option

Source: *Risk Magazine*

Premiums payable for options comprise two elements:
- **intrinsic value**
- **time value**

When LIBOR rises above 5.20 per cent, and if the buyer exercises the option when it is in the money, the payment is the difference between LIBOR and 5.20 per cent. The seller – or writer – of the call option benefits from the payoff. He receives a premium in an agreed currency of 60 basis points, and is not obliged to pay anything until LIBOR reaches 5.20 per cent.

The second diagram in figure 7.2 shows the payoff on a put option. In the figure it is struck when Libor is 4.50 per cent. The buyer is paying 20 basis points for a contract that is out of the money when LIBOR is above 4.50 per cent. It is in the money when LIBOR is below 4.50 per cent. The seller's exposure is again shown by the horizontal line.

Figure 7.3 shows unhedged and hedged exposure involving use of a cap. This alters the borrower's interest rate exposure. The left-hand diagram demonstrates the borrower's short position in LIBOR, the right-hand one the option and underlying combination. There the underlying exposure and the call option combine (the heaviest line in the diagram) to cap the borrower's interest rate at 5.80 per cent. This is the premium plus the strike price. Premiums – similar to value – on options are composed of two elements:

- *Intrinsic value* – the difference between the strike price and the current price of the underlying if it is in the money, or nil if it is out of the money. For example: if the price of the underlying is above the strike price for a call option, exercising the option would net the difference between the two prices (the in the money value). If the price of the underlying is below the strike price, the buyer would not exercise his or her right because the market rate is lower and the underlying can be purchased at that lower rate.

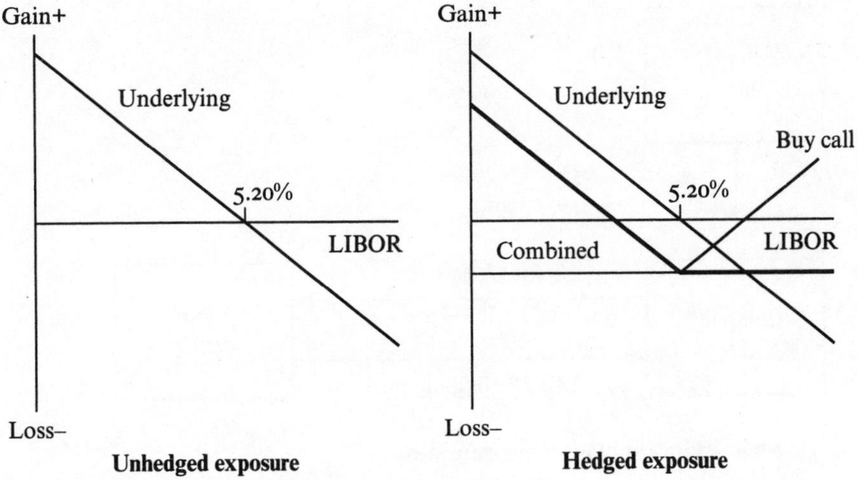

Figure 7.3 Hedged and unhedged exposure using a cap

Source: *Risk Magazine*

- *Time value* – this varies according to a range of factors. The longer the time remaining before an option is exercised the greater the probability that it will be in the money at expiry. This clearly influences the value of the option – which will be higher. The presence of time value means that the price of the option will generally be higher than its intrinsic value.

SOLUTIONS TO INTEREST RATE EXPOSURES

Financing issues such as locking in favourable financing rate opportunities, exploiting favourable rates in other capital markets and retaining positive returns on investments can be profitably managed by using interest rate swaps. The plain vanilla interest rate swap, explained in chapter 5, is the typical corporate choice. AZW Enterprises Inc. borrows from its bank at a floating rate and then swaps this into fixed rate and receives LIBOR in return, as shown in figure 7.4.

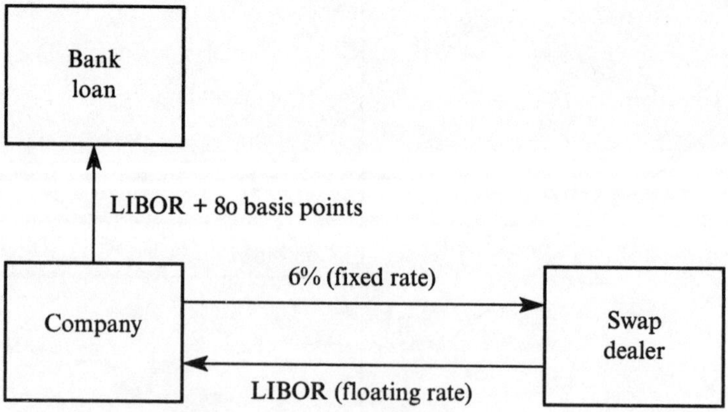

Figure 7.4 Plain vanilla interest rate swap

Source: *Risk Magazine*

AZW might prefer an *interest rate cap*. The company borrows floating-rate debt but it is subject to a fixed upper limit, the cap. Another possibility is a *callable bond*: AZW issues a bond which it can buy back if rates fall below a stated point. In reality, this is a call option on the bond. Yet another way to keep borrowing rates low is to issue *puttable bonds*. The lender can sell the bonds back to the issuer if rates rise above a certain level.

All the solutions described above are excellent possibilities for a case-by-case approach to solving particular exposure problems. A more strategic consideration may require a general examination of the business's overall approach to interest rate exposure. On a closer examination the balance sheet may reveal more floating-rate assets than is at first apparent. Over the business cycle a treasury may prefer more floating-rate than fixed-rate debt. Here protection against rate rises is necessary.

Observing how competitors will be influenced by interest rate movements is important

Observing how competitors will be influenced by interest rate movements is important. A company with mainly floating-rate liabilities will almost certainly benefit when interest rates are falling, especially if rivals have predominantly fixed-rate liabilities. Conversely, the company will be at a disadvantage should interest rates rise when the economy recovers. Competitors that enjoy lower funding costs will be able to attack the company's markets with increased vigour. Hedging against rising rates is therefore something to be given serious consideration.

One way of achieving this is to employ an interest rate collar – to minimise the costs of hedging. If JKL plc is happy with current rates but fears a rise, it may consider an interest rate cap. Caps are expensive, however, so it may be cost effective for JKL to sell an interest rate floor. Here JKL sells put option on rates struck at the floor level, which provides a premium that covers (or offsets) the cost of the cap.

MANAGING CURRENCY EXPOSURES

One standard method of managing currency exposure is to use a currency swap. *Risk Magazine* cites the example of a US paper company planning to open a new plant in Germany:

> The cost will be DM157 million. The company plans to finance the new plant with a US dollar loan from a bank in the United States. Then it will convert the loan into Deutschmarks to build the plant; the company will repay the loan in five years in US dollars. This creates a long position in the Deutschmark: if the DM appreciates, the company will benefit because the DM will buy more dollars; should the DM depreciate, the proceeds will buy fewer dollars.

This clearly creates a currency exposure. A solution involving derivatives would be a currency swap. The following approach would be adopted.

- The company borrows $100 million in the United States.

- It swaps the borrowing for DM157 million – the current exchange rate.
- For five years it uses Deutschmark income from the new plant to pay the fixed DM rate (6.80 per cent).
- It also receives the US dollar fixed rate (7.15 per cent) on the $100 million to offset the payments on the bank loan.

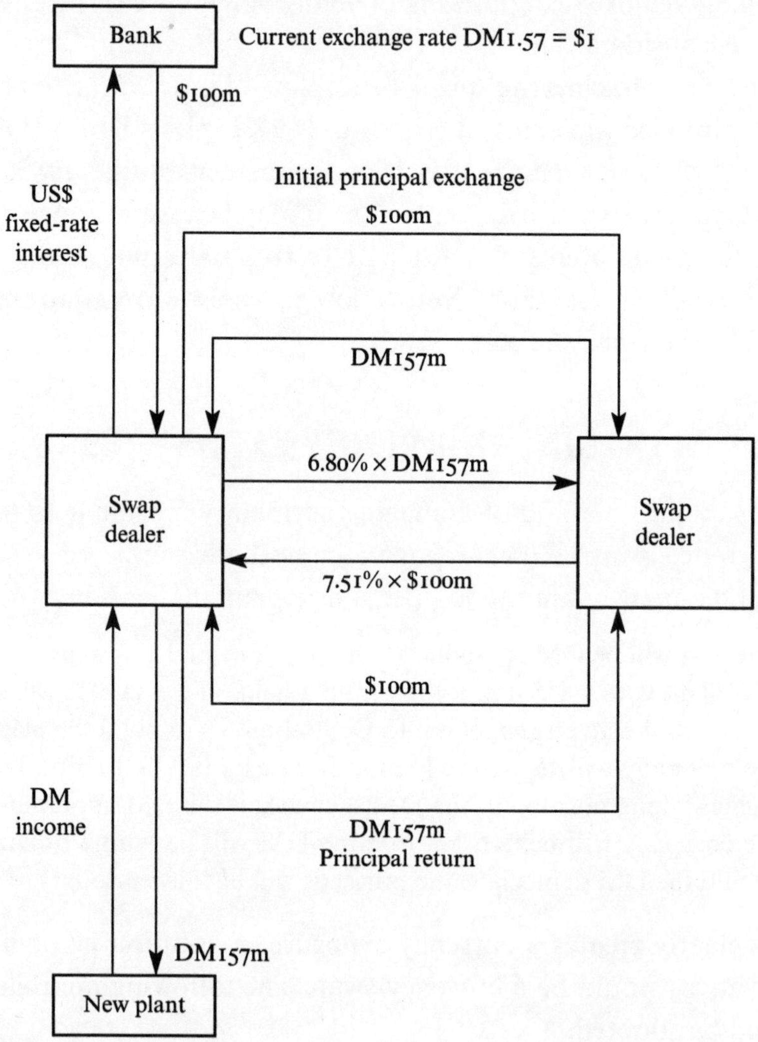

Figure 7.5 Currency swap

Source: *Risk Magazine*

- At the end of the five years the company will repay the DM157 million to the swap dealer.
- It will receive $100 million from the swap dealer to repay the bank loan.

Figure 7.5 sets out this transaction diagrammatically.

Strategic hedging of foreign exchange exposure

The strategic implication of the transaction outlined above is that the US paper company has a long position in the Deutschmark. The company can price more competitively when the DM appreciates and anticipated DM cash flows will convert into more dollars.

Even domestic producers and traders are subjected to currency risk. There are three principal reasons for this:

- components may need to be imported;
- other domestic companies may have external income which influences their competitive position;
- external rivals will be influenced by the movement in currency rates.

Example 7.1 shows how this can arise.

Example 7.1

A domestic Canadian company has Japanese rivals – therefore it is subject to currency exposure. If the Canadian dollar appreciates relative to the yen, the company will in effect be short in the dollar and long in the yen. A cross-currency swap may be the solution to offset the strategic impact of the relationship between the two currencies.

The benefits of a swap are limited, so the Canadian company may choose a currency option. It can achieve protection against and benefit from dollar appreciation.

Figure 7.6 shows, first, the exposure unhedged. On the right-hand side the exposure has been hedged with a currency option.

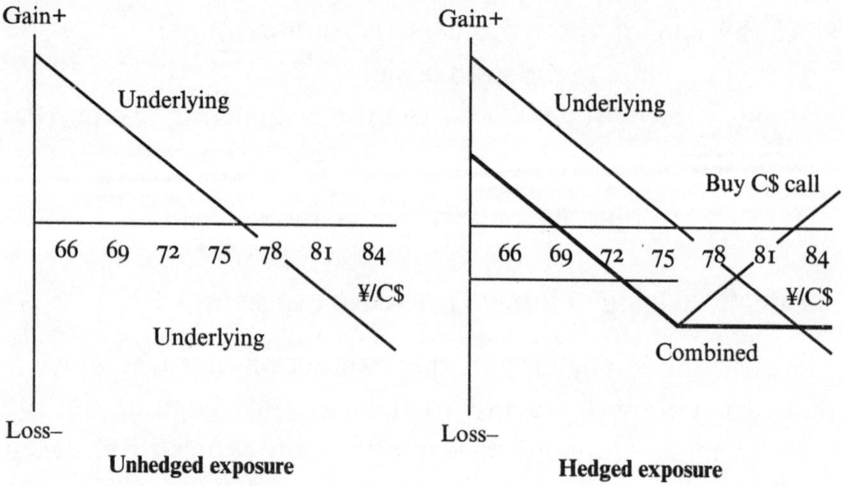

Figure 7.6 Currency option

Source: *Risk Magazine*

The company buys a call on the Canadian dollar and this position limits the losses from appreciation against the yen. If the company has misjudged its exposure, the only penalty will be the option premium .

Range forward contracts

Risk Magazine supplies this example:

> a French company . . . exports within the European Union in a highly competitive, price-sensitive market. The company was comfortable with its competitive exposure to the currency fluctuations permitted within the old Exchange Rate Mechanism. Since the breakdown of the ERM in September 1992, however, the company has been concerned that it will lose market share if the French franc were to appreciate relative to other EC currencies, especially the Deutschmark. The French company's situation, then, is that it is long the Deutschmark; its desired situation is to limit fluctuations in the French franc/Deutschmark rate to those allowed under the old ERM. A low-cost solution is an exchange rate collar, known also as a *range forward* contract, which consists of two parts . . . :

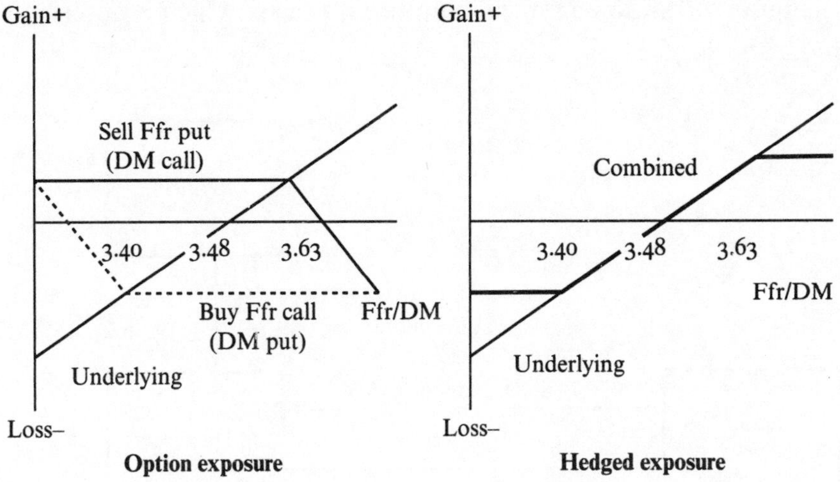

Figure 7.7 Range forward contract

Source: *Risk Magazine*

> (1) writing an out-of-the-money put option on the French franc against the Deutschmark (which is the same as writing a call option on the Deutschmark against the French franc), struck at one end of the desired fluctuation range; and (2) buying an out-of-the-money call option on the French franc against the Deutschmark (put option on the Deutschmark), struck at the other end of the range. The result . . . is that the firm has synthetically reconstructed the exposure it would have had under the old ERM.

Figure 7.7 (also from *Risk Magazine*) explains this example. The left-hand diagram shows the components of the range forward contract, and the right-hand one the result of that contract.

LIMITING COMMODITY EXPOSURES

Futures contracts were – until comparatively recently – the only derivatives tools for dealing with commodity exposures. In the last few years, however, a wide variety of contracts have been tailored to deal with them.

Figure 7.8 shows a typical commodity swap, which is described in Example 7.2.

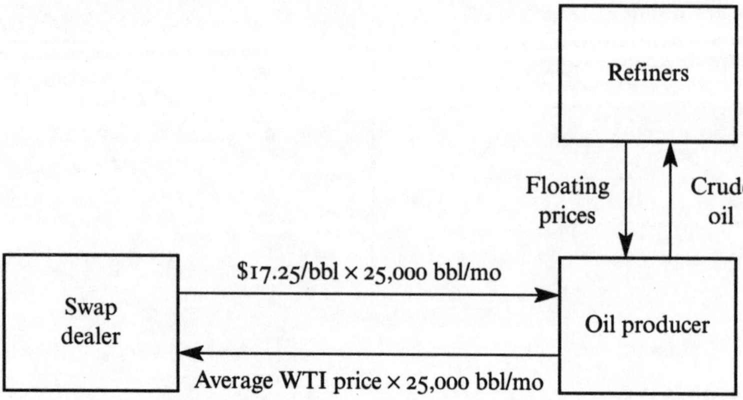

Figure 7.8 Commodities swap

Source: *Risk Magazine*

Example 7.2

An oil company fears competitive disadvantage from variations in the price of crude. The swap dealer pays a fixed price equivalent to $17.25 a barrel a month on 25,000 barrels. In return the oil company pays the average monthly settlement price of West Texas Intermediate (WTI) on the NYMEX exchange.

Figure 7.9 shows another common transaction – the commodity price floor. The form of option used most often for floors and caps is an Asian, or average price, option. The strike price is based on the average of prices over an agreed period. This type of option provides a superior hedge for firms which trade continually – and they cost less than standard options.

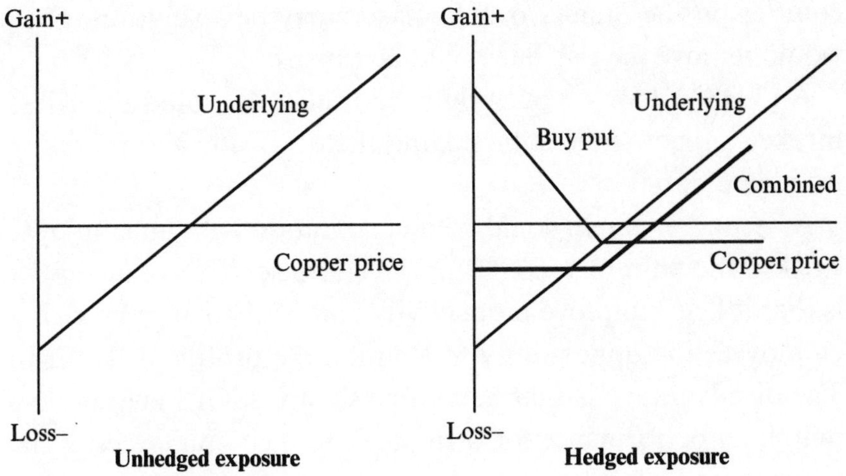

Figure 7.9 Commodity floor

Source: *Risk Magazine*

EQUITY EXPOSURES AND THEIR MANAGEMENT

> ***Equity exposures are often spread throughout a company***

More than any other form of exposure, equity exposures are often spread throughout a company and it is very difficult to determine which the business wants to retain and which it wishes to hedge against. Equity derivatives are among the latest forms of derivatives products and include:

- options on stock indices;
- equity warrants;
- equity swaps.

Solutions vary a great deal and can include a range of possibilities. Say, for instance, that a US fund wants to limit the effect of a fall in equity portfolio values but still wishes to benefit from market price increases. Exchange-traded puts based on equities on the Standard & Poor 500 may be a solution. They would remove the risk but would be expensive.

An OTC S&P 500 put might be useful. It would offer less market impact while still hedging the downside and retaining upside potential.

A second example could be a corporation with an employee stock ownership plan (ESOP). The strategic value of an ESOP is that it helps improve productivity and performance by giving employees the opportunity to share in the profits of the firm. The disadvantage is that many firms with ESOPs guarantee a minimum performance for their stock to their employees: if the stock were to fall, the firm would be faced with the costs of meeting its guarantee. In other words, the firm is implicitly short a put option on its own stock, and faces downside risk if the price were to fall as part of a general market stock decline. A corporation may not be allowed to hedge this risk by means of buying puts on its own stock because of the inherent conflict of interest. An alternative is to hedge out the general market risk by buying an OTC put on the S&P 500. The derivative solution decreases its equity exposure by unbundling the market risk from the risk unique to the firm.

USES OF DERIVATIVES

Corporations use derivatives in specific ways:

- To achieve lower funding costs through arbitrage or customised instruments – these exploit differences between markets. Where financial markets are segmented nationally or internationally, derivatives deliver indisputable cost savings for borrowers and higher yields for investors. See, for example, the currency swap described in figure 7.5.
- Diversifying funding sources – companies can obtain finance from one market; they then swap all or part of the cash flows

into desired currency denominations and rate indices. Placing debt with new investors may increase liquidity and reduce funding costs for the issuer.

- Funding operations in multiple countries at lowest cost – multinationals may find that local borrowing is too small to raise in national markets. It may be more cost effective to borrow more than they need in such markets and swap excess debt into other needed currencies.
- Hedging the cost of future fixed-rate debt – companies may be concerned about volatile interest rates when considering the future cost of fixed-rate debt. Delayed-start swaps or forward swaps could fix the interest rate at the time of the funding decision.
- Hedging the cost of future floating-rate debt – risk here could be limited by using a cap or a swap. In 1990 the publication *Corporate Cashflow* cited the examples of Ocean Spray, makers of cranberry-based products, and Muzak, provider of office music. Ocean Spray has large seasonal borrowing requirements. It used floating-rate borrowings for this purpose but it hedged with a cap to take advantage of any falling rates. Muzak used a two-year collar when it refinanced some floating-rate debt. The company wanted to protect itself against substantially higher rates but to reduce the cost of a cap. At the same time it sold a floor.
- More than 82 per cent of corporations use derivatives to hedge against market risks. Managing existing debt or asset portfolios, interest rate swaps can be used to adjust the ratio of fixed- to floating-rate debt. Currency swaps can transform an obligation in one currency to an obligation in another to change the mix of the currency portfolio.

Learning points

1 Derivatives offer flexibility in dealing with business risk.

2 The variety of solutions available to derivatives buyers has increased dramatically in recent years. The array of underlyings and the scope of applications grow year on year.

3 Common problems identified are interest rate, currency rate, commodity price and equity price exposure.

4 For some of the more straightforward problems swaps are highly relevant. For more complex issues options may be a more effective solution.

8

HOW TO MANAGE THE EFFECTIVENESS OF DERIVATIVES

SUMMARY

This chapter looks at ways of managing derivatives and their effectiveness:

- **the extent of the capacity of the end-users to manage risk**
- **what uses derivatives are put to**
- **key questions to ask treasury managers**
- **how derivatives risk is quantified**
- **risk model systems**
- **the main classifications of derivatives risk**
- **market risk**
- **credit risk**
- **establishing risk-management systems**
- **the need for education in derivatives**

'Directors concerned about . . . derivatives trading may find it worth going back to basics'

'Derivatives can appear an immensely attractive way of killing two birds with one stone'

'[there] emerges a clearly expressed need among end-users for greater education'

In December 1994 the Group of 30 published the results of its survey, undertaken in September 1994, of derivatives at work. The next chapter examines the conclusions of that report – and the implications of its findings for the future of the industry.

Two of its key conclusions have a direct bearing on the management of derivatives positions and portfolios, and the approach taken by directors in understanding their risk profiles. On 7 December 1994 the *Financial Times* discussed the G30 report's implications for end-users. The study:

Managers are now trying to monitor their treasury operations more closely

> found that managers are now trying to monitor their treasury operations more closely. More now review risk management policies than 18 months ago, when the public debate over the use of derivatives started to grow. Others plan to implement stricter internal controls within the next year, as well as introducing fresh risk management guidelines.

Nevertheless, in their *Financial Times* article John Gapper and Richard Waters reported:

> Some boards of directors have been more worried about their treasuries adopting high-risk investment strategies than whether they use derivatives to do so. But there is a second cause of unease . . . that even treasuries of companies may not fully understand the risks they are taking.
>
> The G30 study found that only eight per cent of users said they had adopted the value at risk (VAR) method [see later in this chapter] of calculating how much they stood to lose from market movements when buying derivatives – a method used by sophisticated traders to monitor their portfolios.

HEDGING OR SPECULATION?

The *Financial Times* argued that 'this has disturbing implications, if companies which think they are using derivatives for hedging purposes find they are taking a much riskier leveraged bet on which the losses could be substantial. If more users carried out complex tests on derivatives – such as stress tests showing price movements in conditions of market volatility – it would make it easier to avoid unwanted risks.' Gapper and Waters suggest that a key difficulty exists because end-users cannot obtain access to the risk-management models of the biggest banks. Dealers anticipate that this will change and banks will be more willing to share their software with clients. JP Morgan set the trend with its free risk-management tools package issued in 1994 (see chapter 9).

FIRST STEPS

Directors concerned about any aspects of their derivatives trading may find it worth going back to basics. Executives should attempt to discover the nature and purpose of their derivatives activity. In companies where the scope of derivatives trading is the remit of the treasury team it may prove profitable to ask a few elementary questions. It would be remarkable if non-finance directors did not know if the treasury was using derivatives but they may well not fully understand why derivatives are being used or know which types of the many varieties of products have been selected.

Ask a few elementary questions

Among the first questions which require answers from the treasury team are:

- Why are we using derivatives?
- What do we hope to achieve by using these products?
- Which types of derivatives have we selected and why?

Responses to these questions may provide a brief outline of the nature of the packages being used and why they are being employed. It is worth bearing in mind that, as outlined in earlier chapters, there are two principal reasons for using derivatives: hedging and speculation. Most end-users claim to use derivatives solely for risk management – but financial management policies within their businesses may tell a different story. Increasingly, treasuries are expected to be independent profit centres rather than just an overhead. Derivatives can appear an immensely attractive way of killing two birds with one stone: identified risk can be managed, and there can be a short-term and sometimes highly lucrative return on derivatives. Other forms of risk management, such as debt instruments or insurance, will involve costs which are not refundable. Derivatives products are highly expensive but they cover the risk and pay out a benefit – if they are properly managed.

> **The two principal reasons for using derivatives:**
> - **hedging**
> - **speculation**

> ***The choice of particular products is crucial***

The choice of particular products is crucial. Some, as mentioned earlier, are now commonplace – even standard – in the range of financial instruments. The simpler forms of forwards and swaps have been used for more than twenty years. Options are often more complicated and some – while being the most appropriate technique to use in certain circumstances – can place heavy pressure on treasuries in terms of measuring and monitoring their risk profile.

MANAGEMENT OF THE RISKS

Directors need to understand clearly which risks are being managed and whether derivatives are the most effective way of handling such risks. They need to be conversant with the approaches available for potentially managing such risks (see chapter 3). Derivatives represent only one of a number of such approaches.

Questions which could be asked to elicit and understand this information include:

- What are the risks and what techniques are available for managing them?
- To what extent is the portfolio risk managed with derivatives products?
- What risk-management policies are in place for managing the risks inherent in the application of derivatives for this purpose?
- To what extent has the board approved the management of this risk?
- What methodologies are used by the treasury to measure and monitor risk? Is value at risk (VAR) the preferred method?

The checklist that follows establishes a number of more pointed enquiries.

Checklist for testing the effectiveness of derivatives

This is a set of questions for directors managing departments which use and operate derivatives.

- **Do you know what you are trying to achieve in your use of derivatives? In particular, have you set formal objectives and policies?**
- **Do you regard derivatives activity as peripheral or integral to our business activities ?**
- **Is treasury activity in general – and derivatives activity in particular – adequately reported?**
- **Can you measure and monitor the financial risk (including the risk effects of derivatives)?**

- **Is there adequate segregation of duties in your treasury function and in finance/accounts to ensure that all derivatives activity undertaken is captured and reported?**
- **Do the people in your treasury have sufficient training and experience to cope with all aspects of your derivatives activity?**
- **Can your treasury systems adequately process all of the derivatives that you undertake?**
- **To what extent are you writing options and why?**
- **What are the procedures for obtaining tax and accounting sign-offs on derivatives activities?**
- **How will you know if something is going wrong? Do you have a set of procedures for dealing with such problems if they occur?**

THE MANAGEMENT OF RISK IN DERIVATIVES

Four types of risk *must* be identified and then managed:
- **market risk**
- **credit risk**
- **operational risk**
- **legal risk**

The additional exposure created by the device adopted to manage the risk must also be managed in just the same way as the main risk itself. The G30 1993 report, which first identified the nature and extent of the risk-management issue, identified four areas which should be managed:

- market risk;
- credit risk;
- operational risk;
- legal risk.

Market risk and credit risk require greater attention because they are the areas of highest potential loss. They are also easier to identify. Three basic questions need to be answered:

- What is a portfolio worth in today's market?
- How sensitive is the portfolio to market changes?
- How much would be lost if a counterparty were to default?

Operational risk is largely a matter of internal control and legal risk should be contained by proper documentation.

MARKING TO MARKET

The G30 report suggested that derivatives should be valued by marking to market. This shows how the value of a hedge has changed in relation to that of the underlying security; whether the hedge is still appropriate. It also provides a starting point from which to measure market risk by showing how the hedge has changed against moving market conditions.

The process of marking OTC products to market begins with computing three sets of interest rates (for exchange-traded products one looks up the price; similarly where the underlying is, for example, equities or commodities):

- the yield curve for coupon bonds, specifically the on-the-run yield curve for newly issued debt;
- a zero-coupon yield curve on instruments which pay no cash until maturity;
- the implied forward yield curve on money borrowed at some stage in the future. This is used to estimate floating rates to be paid in the future.

These computations are then applied to specific circumstances regarding particular products.

Forwards and swaps

Marking swaps and forwards to market is done done by determining the net present value of the future cash flows. This is equal to the difference between the present value of cash inflows and cash outflows. At the start of the contract this value is normally zero, because cash flows are in balance and value grows or declines from this point. As the market moves the value may be either:

- positive (in the money); or
- negative (out of the money).

Values change differently on either side of the contract. On the fixed side, cash flows do not change but the rate at which the market discounts them does. On the floating side the cash flows do change. This means that they must be recomputed at the new rate.

Options

Options require a more complex pricing model than that for forwards and swaps. The most well-known and widely applied is the Black–Scholes model. This can be programmed into a pocket calculator and is useful for the less complicated calculations. Its limitations can be summarised succinctly:

- it is only for expiry figures; and therefore
- it is suitable only for European-style options.

Options require a more complex pricing model

Most options are American-style and can therefore be exercised at any stage before expiry. Equally, problems can arise with interest rate options. The model assumes that volatility in the underlying is constant throughout the life of the option. A different issue exists with bond options, whose volatility decreases as the option approaches maturity.

Phil Rivett and Peter Speak in *The Financial Jungle* describe the Black–Scholes model:

This [i.e. Black–Scholes] and other models which have been developed subsequently are based on the concept of the riskless or neutral hedge. The concept is derived from the risk equivalence of the combinations of positions in options and the underlying transaction . . . The riskless hedge concept requires that, subject to a number of assumptions, a perfectly hedged position consisting of a long position in an underlying stock and a short position in options on that stock (or a long position on the options and a short position in the stock) can be constructed. This position is perfectly hedged because, for a range of stock prices close to the current price, any profit resulting from the increase in price of the stock would be offset by a loss on the option, and vice versa. In this way, options can completely eliminate market risk from a stock portfolio. If there were no transaction costs, the hedged position could be amended constantly to keep the portfolio risk-free. Therefore, the option premium at which the hedge yields a pretax rate of return equivalent to the risk free rate is the fair value of the option.

Example of Black–Scholes model

The Black–Scholes model is mathematically complex, but the riskless hedge concept can be shown using the following example:

Suppose that the ordinary shares of ABC plc are trading at £5 per share, and the price of the shares can rise or fall in each year by only £1. An investor wishes to establish the fair value of a European call option with a strike price of £3 which expires at the end of the year. To construct the riskless hedge, a portfolio long one share and hedged by short positions in call options has to be constructed. The number of calls required to do this is calculated as follows:

> The price of the share is currently £5. At the end of the year the price can rise to £6 or fall to £4. If the price rises to £6, the writer of the option will lose £3 (6 – 3). If the price falls to £4 the writer will lose £1. The number of calls required ('C') for a riskless portfolio can be calculated by equating the two possible price movements:
>
> $6 - (C \times 3) = 4 - (C \times 1)$
>
> Therefore, the number of calls (C) = 1

This portfolio is riskless because if the share price rises to £6, the total value of the portfolio will be £3, that is equal to the value of the share (£6), less the loss on the call option of £3. Similarly, if the share price falls to £4, the value of the share of £4 will be offset by a loss on the call option of £1, a total value for the portfolio of £3. If the share price remains at £5 the total value of the portfolio is also £3 (share price £5 less loss on call option of £2 (5 – 3)).

As this portfolio is risk free, it must earn the equivalent of the risk free rate of interest (if it did not, arbitrage would bring it into line).

Therefore the portfolio must have a value at the beginning of the year equal to its closing value discounted at the risk free rate of interest. However the cost of the portfolio is also equal to the price paid for the share less the premium received for the call option ('P'). If the risk free rate of interest for the period is 10% the premium for the option can be calculated as follows:

$$\frac{3}{1.10} = (5 - P)$$

Therefore, P, the premium on the call is £2.27

The most important assumptions which have been made in the above example are:

- the call option has European exercise terms and no dividends are paid on the underlying share;
- transaction costs have been ignored;
- a single risk free interest rate for the period to expiry of the option is used. Investors cannot usually borrow and lend at the same rate.

MARKET RISK

This involves determine the sensitivity of a portfolio to changes in the financial markets and then assessing the extent of the exposure to the risks of such changes. The risk must be measured across the entire portfolio and not against individual products. Measuring against individual products can overstate the risk.

There are three elements to the mathematical calculation:

- how large a market change should be assumed;
- the consequent risk to the complete portfolio;
- the time needed to unwind the portfolio.

An increasingly commonly used method, mentioned earlier in this chapter, is value at risk (VAR). This determines the maximum expected loss within a specified period from an adverse movement in markets. VAR involves three steps:

- first, determine past changes in the underlying rate and prices – this gives the standard deviation in daily market movements;
- second, establish a worst-case scenario;
- finally, calculate he potential loss by inserting the worst case into the portfolio valuation and projecting it over the 'unwinding period' (i.e. the span over which a loss can occur).

A full analysis would also take into account movements in abnormal markets. This is probably best achieved by using stress test models (techniques for determining how products perform in abnormal market conditions), which are becoming standard practice.

Additional needs for options

The fundamental principles of assessing market risk apply to options in just the same way as to swaps and forwards. Options behave differently, however, and this makes market risk measurement more complex than with swaps and forwards.

After working out the appropriate factors, it is important to conduct simulations to assess market risks of option portfolios. This is because option risks or price movements relative to the underlying are non-linear.

Once the various calculations described above have been made, management is in a position to begin managing market risk.

The approach must be tailored to suit the needs of a specific treasury. The G30 1993 report encourages management to set risk limits based on such factors as:

- tolerance to low-probability high losses against higher-probability modest losses;
- capital resources;
- market liquidity;
- anticipated profitability of a particular transaction;
- the organisation's trading experience;
- business strategy.

CREDIT RISK

Credit risk comes from counterparty default and for derivatives is related to market risk in that the risk is calculated by reference to price movements in markets. *Risk Magazine*'s *Guide to Corporate Exposure Management* comments:

> Managing credit risk involves both qualitative and quantitative aspects. The qualitative aspect is determining the creditworthiness of counterparties with which a firm will do business. The qualitative aspect involves measuring credit exposure to each counterparty.

The 1993 G30 report suggests two methods for measuring the risk:

- *current exposure* – i.e. the replacement cost of the derivatives;
- *potential exposure* – an estimate of the future replacement cost of derivatives transactions. This is done by using a probability analysis, for example based on two standard deviations over the remaining term of the transaction. The organisation which is managing the risk will determine the most suitable deviations.

Current and potential exposure are inseparable. Current exposure is the mark-to-market exposure: a positive replacement cost is the current credit exposure. If the market value is negative there is no current exposure. To calculate potential exposure, three steps are required:

- Simulate how interest rates might move over the life of the transaction.
- Prepare a forward swap curve to project the fixed rate on swaps in the future. This gives an appreciation of replacement cost.
- Estimate how great a credit exposure would occur as a result of rate changes; only positive replacement costs are pertinent. Credit exposure is measured both as peak exposure – or worst-case scenario – which is the highest level of exposure, and also the expected exposure, which is the average loss anticipated in a given year.

Additional needs for options

The same factors apply in the measurement of the credit risk in options. Buying an option incurs a current credit exposure, which will last until the option is worthless, has expired or is sold. Conversely, selling an option creates no current credit exposure for the seller but an exposure for the buyer. Potential credit exposure is arrived at in the same way as with forwards or swaps. It is analysed using the forward-rate curve to predict future patterns of interest rates and volatility. Estimates of potential losses vary more than for forwards or swaps.

Exposure is identified as either gross or net. Gross adds all positive exposures, net offsets the negative against the positive.

According to *Risk Magazine*, 'the question remains what to do with the analysis. Both qualitative and quantitative information can provide input to management decisions on limits which constrain the concentration of a firm's exposure to a particular counterparty, to a group of counterparties or to a country.'

Selling an option creates no current credit exposure

MANAGING THE RISK

An effective control system should ensure that:

- risk-management duties are properly supervised;
- any segregation of management duties is clearly identified;
- position and risk are coherently reported;
- transactions are properly documented;
- the roles of the players are adequately defined.

Companies need to decide and make clear whether responsibility for certain functions is to be centralised or decentralised. A useful rule is that responsibilities for different functions should be spread.

- The treasury should handle the risk-management strategy.
- Accounting should deal with record keeping, processing and settlement.
- The legal department should arrange contractual relationships.
- The credit control department should deal with the assessment of counterparties.

This is by no means an exhaustive list but it indicates the kind of considerations which should underscore management thinking when deciding on division of responsibilities. It should also help to promote effective teamwork on the issues.

Policies

Management should establish a policy for general risk management and specifically for derivatives usage. It may want to form a risk-management committee to draw up the strategy and monitor its implementation. Any such strategy should be reasonably detailed and specific. Too many generalities can lead to confusion, ambiguity and misinterpretation. A policy to hedge may be stated but without describing what constitutes a hedge or identifying which products may be used.

The treasury should state clearly the nature of the policy it intends to pursue and which products it will use. Communication throughout the organisation is essential so that everyone who needs to know is aware of the strategy.

This strategy should be approved by the executive and board of directors. Meetings should be established to review the strategy with senior management.

GREATER EDUCATION

From surveys completed in the latter half of 1994 emerges a clearly expressed need among end-users for greater education. Dealers may throw up their hands in horror, and point out that they already run courses for clients on derivatives and how they work, but considerable demand already exists for greater depth and coverage. Generally speaking, the courses do not extend to those senior directors who are responsible for shareholders' funds. The annual survey of fund managers in *Derivatives in Fund Management* magazine published in November 1994 in conjunction with Coopers & Lybrand reported that respondents worldwide still regarded education as the primary need.

Michael Levy, who compiled the document, said:

> fund managers consider knowledge and understanding of derivatives, their functions and the risks associated with using them as the key priority. Our previous survey in 1993, which was restricted to Europe, also identified education as a major issue. But it assumed overriding importance in our latest report.

The 1994 survey drew reactions from the United Kingdom (46 per cent), the United States and Canada (24 per cent), continental Europe (18 per cent) and the Asia/Pacific region (12 per cent). Many of the managers of the large funds responded. Levy's report underlines the extent to which end-users regard as vital the need to gain a much fuller knowledge of products they are using routinely but do not fully understand.

Principal findings in the *Derivatives in Fund Management* analysis reflect the research conducted for this book among dealers, regulators and end-users. The magazine also publishes a newsletter, and this reported a series of conclusions. Among them were:

- derivatives are being employed by a broader range of users;
- a wider range of products is being deployed;
- the applications of those products are equally diverse.

However:

- end-users express a preference for simpler derivatives which are easier to deploy and then monitor – swaps, for example, are increasingly seen as a conventional risk-management tool;
- end-users' systems for measuring risk are inadequate;
- one third of managers would like to use more derivatives but their technology comes nowhere near what is needed to exploit any benefits from derivatives products.

Help is at hand, however, and among the collection of moves by regulators and professional bodies is a paper by the UK-based Association of Corporate Treasurers (ACT). The ACT's guidelines for the risk management of derivatives in corporate treasuries suggest that there is little failure of products but an absence of strong controls by companies. The document argues that the succession of losses has encouraged an impression that businesses cannot handle these complicated instruments.

The ACT says that the problem lies not in the complexity of the products but in a failure of control systems at a basic level. Calling for strategic and policy control at board level, the Association suggests that simply to give hedging as the objective of using derivatives is insufficient. Derek Ross, chairman of the ACT technical committee and

The problem lies . . . in a failure of control systems

author of the guidelines, said that hedging is an ambiguous concept which needs to be defined precisely. Treasuries need to understand that hedging is a defined activity which is structured within values and time limits. The worth of the hedge is dictated by several predetermined factors.

The ACT suggests that a basic failure of supervision by companies lies behind the catalogue of losses. It calls for the monitoring and reporting of all derivatives activities plus an internal audit on treasury dealers. A separate risk-management function would ensure compliance with limits to exposure and independent reporting to management.

Treasurers have responded by attacking the proposals as 'over the top', which probably means that they are on the right lines. The treasurers defended derivatives as much maligned but the report was careful to point out, albeit in a limited fashion, that derivatives are generally not the problem. That lies in the control levels and patterns of risk management available to the treasurers.

Levy went even further:

> I recall one highly experienced banker in the States who made a key point which is often misunderstood here. He said that derivatives are emphatically not the problem. The real issue is gearing. Gearing can exist with any financial instruments. Certain products – the more complex options in particular – can expose businesses to very heavy gearing. But derivatives, *per se*, have risks involved but it is only the more exotic brands which expose businesses to unnecessary levels of gearing.

The message appears to be winning some degree of consensus. Nicholas Denton in the derivatives column of the *Financial Times* said:

> there may be no boardroom panic but there is concern. For a start about one tenth of UK treasury departments still trade for profit

> and that can also expose them more to losses. Speculating treasurers can always do damage but highly leveraged derivatives can allow them to wreak havoc. It is possible to lose money on a standard but misjudged derivative. A company can misjudge its underlying exposure. It could, for example, overestimate its sensitivity to interest rate movements and overcompensate. And some corporate treasurers will experiment with complicated instruments which are beyond them.

However, some corporations are responding to the wave of losses with significant steps. Among the measures introduced recently have been:

- more board-level control of treasury policy;
- restrictions on the usage of certain instruments;
- controls on the treasury activities of rogue subsidiaries where many of the derivatives losses have occurred;
- a general move from exotica to plain vanilla swaps;
- workshops and seminars on derivatives.

Learning points

1 Risk must be managed – the penalty can be extremely harsh if it is not.

2 The management of risk involves:

(a) setting board-level guidelines covering the extent and the nature of the risk an organisation is prepared to take;
(b) specifying who is responsible for risk management and detailing the extent of his, her or their responsibility;
(c) deciding on the extent to which the organisation wishes to deal in derivatives and ensuring that appropriate risk-management systems are in place to monitor them.

3 It is particularly important to make quite clear whether derivatives are to be used for hedging or speculation.

4 Systems must seek to manage market risk, credit risk, operational risk and legal risk.

5 Various risk-management models exist; the best is probably value at risk (VAR).

9

THE FUTURE

SUMMARY

This chapter examines the future for the derivatives trader and end-user. It looks at the following points:

- the likely challenges for the derivatives industry
- the impact of the Group of 30 in improving standards among dealers and end-users
- the renewed focus on improving risk-management techniques
- the growth and potential growth of Pacific Rim and Latin American exchanges
- advances in dealing/end-user technology and how they will change the derivatives market
- why and how end-users are becoming more knowledgeable about their derivatives exposure
- the pattern of development of new products

‘[In 1994] systems at the banks and at end-users were . . . substantially inadequate’

‘in 1994 . . . TIFFE was the second-fastest-growing exchange in the world’

‘the “rocket scientists” are preparing to take the concept of derivatives still further’

In chapter 1 we discussed the rapid growth of derivatives, the increasing range of their application and the globalisation of trading in derivatives products. During 1994 regulators, banks and end-user organisations emphasised the improvement of risk-management systems among traders and buyers of products. They concurred, however, that while systems had progressed from what had been a low level of operating efficiency they still had a considerable distance to travel before they would be adequate for the task. This should be set against an environment where new derivatives – some of them even more complex – were being developed on a regular basis. Using 1994 as a standard, systems at the banks and at end-users were therefore substantially inadequate.

Each has argued – in the face of heavy criticism – that derivatives products are not at fault. They are advanced as inherently sound, but two issues which influence their useful application predominate. First, a weakness exists in the trading houses which deal in these products. Levels of training in the banks – especially among sales staff – vary widely. This can lead them to focus on achieving ambitious targets to the detriment of the quality of the solutions they provide to end-users. Thus, end-users – who may not realise the extent of the risk to which they are exposed by certain derivatives products – are sold packages which may appear, at first glance, to be suitable.

Later it becomes abundantly clear that buyers did not possess even the most elementary understanding of how these products work, let alone the risks they entail. There have been examples of end-users suffering devastating losses after being sold products of which neither they nor the trader have any real appreciation. If any prescriptive regulation is introduced by the US Congress in the coming months it may focus on those clients such as local authorities which have little capacity to assess realistically what they are being sold.

The second area, which may be the subject of even greater debate, is risk-management systems. The Group of 30's December 1994 survey of industry risk-management provision reported that further work needed to be done among dealers, treasuries and end-users to enhance risk-management measurement and systems. Substantial improvements had been achieved – especially by dealers – by benchmarking against the guidelines outlined in the previous, 1993 G30 survey.

The rumpus over large losses, the pressure by politicians – especially in Congress – and the response by senior industry practitioners in dialogue with regulators have elevated the quality of discussion and performance by all sides in the sector. There is unanimity that derivatives are significant players in the economic environment, that many of the simpler products have become conventional financial/risk-management tools and that these instruments will not disappear just because of failures in their application and management. In the United States the publication, in March 1995, of a 'Framework for Voluntary Oversight' by the Derivatives Policy Group (which comprises six leading US derivatives houses) goes some way towards providing regulation on a voluntary basis. It will be interesting to see if this framework gains widespread acceptance. Its management controls summary is contained in Appendix III.

These instruments will not disappear just because of failures in their application

THE 1994 G30 REPORT

The Group of 30's 1994 report represented a step forward. Its 1993 recommendations were recognised by the industry as a whole as setting the standard. Following the 1993 report dealers, treasuries and end-users – even if they were not able to comply with its findings – had announced their intention of reviewing their systems and procedures.

The introduction to the 1994 report explains that the 1994 survey had been the most comprehensive survey of the principles and practice of derivatives undertaken throughout the world:

> This report contains the findings of two questionnaire surveys on risk management practices for derivatives. In September 1994 the surveys were sent to roughly 900 firms worldwide – to approximately 300 dealers of over-the-counter derivatives and one to approximately 600 end-users. Of these, 125 dealers and 149 end-users responded.

Although the responses of 274 dealers and end-users are not conclusive they do give a strong impression of the direction of developments in these markets. The response rate is high statistically but the results do pose a secondary question: the extent to which respondents represent the more forward-looking element of the sample. It would be surprising if any of the 900 firms of dealers issued with the questionnaires were not familiar with the recommendations contained in the G30's 1993 report but there is still widespread ignorance among end-users.

The summary of responses shows the level of improvement among both dealers and end-users: '58 per cent of the dealers have already used the 1993 survey to benchmark their own risk management practices. Another 30 per cent plan to do so in the next 12 months. Among end-users 33 per cent have already used the recommendations for benchmarking and another 16 per cent plan to do so over the next year.'

'only one-twelfth of end-users actively evaluate their systems against G30 guidelines'

The 1993 recommendations had called for:

- better risk-management systems for dealers and end-users;
- greater accountability for derivatives transactions;
- improved training for sales personnel and end-users;
- enhanced policy guidelines for derivatives transactions;
- procedures for derivatives transactions to be approved by boards of directors;
- enhanced review procedures for involvement in derivatives;
- greater consistency and thoroughness in measurement of derivatives activities;
- improved professional expertise in the conduct of transactions;
- greater transparency in accounting procedures and wider disclosure.

The 1994 survey reported considerable advances among dealers using stress tests (to determine a product's performance in abnormal market conditions) on their portfolios. In July 1993 only 19 per cent of dealers used them. A further 35 per cent adopted such programmes in the period of 15 months following the survey and an additional 39 per cent planned to introduce stress tests before the end of 1995.

THE KEY FINDINGS OF THE 1994 G30 SURVEY

It is important to emphasise that fewer than 50 per cent of the dealers' sample replied. The conclusions should therefore be judged with a measure of detachment.

The key findings of the survey were classified into three categories:

- market making by dealers;
- treasury activities by dealers;
- treasury activities by commercial and financial end-users.

Market making by dealers

All dealers who responded thought that the G30's 1993 recommendations were useful and relevant to the management of their businesses. The key findings were that:

- 88 per cent reported that senior management plan to benchmark their risk-exposure practices against the G30 recommendations;
- almost all respondents said that senior management currently review and approve derivatives risk-management policies and procedures (a rise of 25 per cent on 1993);
- 93 per cent of boards of management now review and approve overall risk-management and capital policies (this represents an improvement of almost 30 per cent over 1993);
- 91 per cent mark to market daily;
- 98 per cent of the largest dealers and 83 per cent of all dealers formally measure and compare risk exposures against established limits on a daily basis;
- value at risk (VAR – see chapter 8) is preferred by 43 per cent of all dealers, with a further 37 per cent intending to adopt VAR by the end of 1995 (the figures for large dealers are 58 and 38 per cent respectively);
- 80 per cent measure current credit exposure using replacement cost of derivatives transactions; a further 15 per cent plan to do so within twelve months;
- 97 per cent use independent credit-risk management functions;
- 84 per cent have independent market-risk management functions; another 14 per cent intend to introduce them during 1995;
- 51 per cent use netting (see chapter 10) for credit-risk management; a further 45 per cent plan to do so in 1995;
- 54 per cent of all dealers perform stress simulations to assess how portfolios will perform under abnormal conditions, a level which should rise to 93 per cent during 1995 (for the largest firms the percentages are 60 and 96 respectively);

- mark-to-market accounting is used by 83 per cent of firms handling between 2,500 and 10,000 transaction a year (a rise of 21 per cent over July 1993). Among firms handling fewer than 2,500 transactions a year these techniques are used by 78 per cent – a rise of 23 per cent.

Perhaps less impressive, however, fewer than half of all dealers' independent credit- and market-risk functions ensure that there is an integrated approach to technology.

Treasury activities by dealers

Dealers (largely in the major banks) also undertake treasury activities for their own institutions. In such cases the applicability of the G30's 1993 recommendations appeared to depend on the size of firm. Larger firms, in the main, had more extensive functions. The 1994 survey found that:

- 88 per cent of firms said that management had implemented risk-management policies for non-dealing derivatives activities;
- 79 per cent of dealers mark to market some or all of their derivatives positions at least once a month;
- 38 per cent of the largest firms currently use VAR.

End-users

In the third category – the (largely US) end-users – the main findings of the survey were that:

- 40 per cent of firms measure the extent and nature of market risk on the basis of a maximum loss in a specific scenario, and set limits accordingly;
- 31 per cent, alternatively, use sensitivity to additional basis points move;
- 42 per cent perform stress simulations for abnormal situations; 19 per cent more plan to in 1995;

- 39 per cent of all firms – and 70 per cent of larger businesses – have independent risk-management functions;
- 64 per cent of all businesses – 85 per cent of larger ones – measure credit exposure using replacement cost;
- 90 per cent designate the individual who is responsible for committing the company to derivatives transactions and clearly communicate this within the organisation; some 6 per cent more plan to in 1995;
- 48 per cent of all companies disclose qualitative information about their derivatives transactions. This climbs to 65 per cent among larger businesses.

Some implications of the survey findings

The percentage implementation or forecast implementation figures for dealers are higher than those for end-users – but dealers started from a higher base. This does not alter the fact that end-users appear to have rather more work to do. This view is supported by the lower percentage findings and lower level of returns from end-users. However, the findings are balanced by the fact that dealers need to have more advanced systems, greater professional expertise and policies in greater depth. Volumes in trading houses vastly exceed those of even the largest end-users. The need for daily marking to market, for example, is absolute in dealing houses but may be less pressing for end-users – depending on the extent of their derivatives portfolios.

The G30 figures are useful for the following reasons:

- they show the trend of development in the sector;
- they highlight the key areas of concern;
- they show that dealers' risk-management techniques and functions are considerably more sophisticated than are the end-users';
- they demonstrate the areas requiring further attention and

improvement – for example, end-user training, the need for end-users to formulate a derivatives policy, and the importance of clear communication within end-user organisations.

TO LEGISLATE OR NOT TO LEGISLATE

Despite the cheering news of the G30 report and the partnership developed between regulators and dealers to provide self-regulation, the industry still came in for considerable criticism in 1994. Cumulative losses related to the sector reached $6 billion. Regardless of the maturity of the derivatives industry – especially in the United States – a profound misunderstanding about the risk profile of specific products continued to create problems.

A General Audit Office report on the sector (which the industry had hoped would give a balanced perspective) was viewed by many as a missed opportunity. Three large corporate users – Procter & Gamble, Equity Group Holdings and Gibson Greetings – took Bankers Trust to court to seek to recover more than $200 million in damages for derivatives losses. Bankers Trust – a name synonymous with derivatives – is adamant in refuting claims that it did not fully explain the risks in its products, which are even more complex than most derivatives. Gibson Greetings and Bankers Trust have since settled their action.

In 1994 losses related to the sector reached $6 billion

In this climate the growth in product volumes in the key Chicago and New York futures exchanges began to level out. No longer was the rapid rise in derivatives transactions seen, and in November 1994 distinguished commentators were arguing that the markets in these principal cities were 'maturing'. Although volumes in Europe were pushing through the ceiling, the head of the Frankfurt futures exchange was arguing that there were too many exchanges in the region. He said that with twenty exchanges offering futures products there would not be enough business to go around. *The Economist*'s annual review, *The World In Figures 1995*, was so concerned about the lack of understanding among purchasers of derivatives that it commented: 'ignorance among end-users will cause more calamities in 1995'.

Yet 1994 will probably be seen as a positive turning point for derivatives. The threat of destructive and penal legislation in the United States – where more than half of all trades currently take place – has receded. The regulators have come to perceive – presumably as a result of effective lobbying by the banks – derivatives as a beneficial force for the global economy. They do make a useful contribution to the management of risk and, properly handled, can enhance the efficiency of businesses. Even Alan Greenspan, chairman of the Federal Reserve, has gone on record to indicate that derivatives increase economic efficiency.

In the *Financial Times*'s annual survey of trends in the derivatives industry, journalist Patrick Harverson remarked: 'the fear among US bankers and regulators alike is that if lawmakers introduce legislation tightening federal regulation of derivatives dealers, the market's growth could be badly undermined'. He cited Joseph Lynyak, head of the American Bar Association's banking committee on derivatives, who concluded that 'the question is whether they are going to throw the baby out with the bath water, and perceive derivatives to be such a problem that they over regulate the business to the point where they destroy the market'. Harverson's synopsis argues that since summer 1994 regulators have been telling Congress legislators in a series of hearings on derivatives that present regulation is appropriate to the task and

Derivatives increase economic efficiency

that self-regulation is preferable to prescriptive over-regulation. The regulators linked hands with the traders at a time when end-users were experiencing weak knees and legislators were emboldened following a tidal wave of bad publicity about the industry.

The leading advocates in Congress for legislation to ring-fence derivatives activities – Henry Gonzalez, Jim Leach and Edward Markey – seemed determined to press ahead with proposals to tighten derivatives supervision when Congress reconvened in January 1995. But the unholy alliance of regulators and traders seemed highly sanguine about its prospects. Senior industry advisers told Harverson that legislators were expected to introduce legislation in the new Congress but that 'what's curious about it is that there seems to be no support for legislation beyond a few individuals'.

On 19 November 1994 *The Economist* expressed an even more bullish opinion, which must have encouraged the traders' party:

> Much of the new [Congress] agenda will be set by the House [of Representatives'] banking committee, which will be led by Jim Leach. Alfonse D'Amato, the new chairman of the Senate banking committee, will be too busy pursuing his Whitewater prey to worry about the minutiae of financial reform.
>
> Mr Leach on the other hand is brimming with ideas. His top priority is to scrap parts of the Glass–Steagall Act that separates commercial from investment banking in America . . . And he would also like to streamline the financial industry's tangled regulatory system. Encouragingly, Mr Leach also thinks that futures, options and other derivatives are good for commerce. Rather than producing detailed legislation to govern their use, he would like to give more power to regulators to develop whatever supervisory standards for the industry they see fit.

The newspaper's analysis said that reform would be dependent on structural changes in Congress. Delays in the present process could be removed by the newly ascendant Republicans, which would make the legislative path easier to pursue.

If *The Economist* – and other respected commentators – are correct the focus of attention will shift back to the regulators. And they have not been slow. National and international agencies have been hard at work launching enquiries and setting out proposed guidelines on a raft of related issues. It is arguable that the recommendations for self-regulation they have been advancing will obviate the need for Congress to take any precipitate steps toward draconian legislation. They have proposed new rules which will enhance the existing reporting machinery, and the accounting and disclosure requirements for dealers and end-users. Among the US agencies which have been introduced recommendations or initiated enquiries into such activities are:

- the Office of the Comptroller of the Currency, which is the Treasury's bank regulation division;
- the Securities and Exchange Commission, regulator of the securities firms;
- the Commodity Futures Trade Commission, which oversees exchange-traded derivatives;
- the Financial Standards Accounting Board, pressing for greater corporate disclosure about derivatives holdings.

Clearly, this package of regulator-inspired initiatives will act for the good, whatever Capitol Hill decides to do. Joseph Lynyak, in the *Financial Times*, forecast: 'what you are going to see is probably some minor accounting changes, some securities disclosure, and some capital requirements from the Basle committee'.

Earlier we referred to the nature of the BIS committee's. These are setting the pace of the international debate on improving the regulation, reporting and risk management of derivatives. In July 1994 the Basle committee (of the Bank of International Settlements – BIS) and the International Organisation of Securities Commissions (IOSCO) together published guidelines which called for stronger internal risk management of derivatives trading by banks and securities houses. The Basle committee did not let the grass grow under its feet, and in October 1994 issued new standards requiring dealers to disclose more about inherent derivatives risks and to establish substantially improved systems for monitoring, measuring and handling such risks.

There is now widespread demand among regulators – and indeed among the reputable dealers – for international co-ordination of standards to improve self-regulation of accounting, disclosure and risk-management systems. In 1995 the Basle committee set the levels of capital adequacy – assets in reserve that banks must retain against trading risks. Given the momentum banks have managed to develop, they will probably be able to win the argument over which basis to use for the new capital-adequacy standard. Their internal value-at-risk (VAR) models will probably be the preferred choice. This solution is not without its downsides. Regulators may not be able to validate some of the VAR models, merely acknowledge or recognise them. Approval will entail imposing some degree of liability on the individual supervisor as well as on the institution itself if things go wrong. National supervisory teams which are inexperienced in inspections at individual banks and auditors could be hamstrung if obliged to conduct such investigations. Their task will be made all the more difficult because VAR models are normally constructed based on out-of-date information and outdated criteria. This would be a problem in most banking activities – in derivatives management it is especially acute.

The relationship between the Basle committee of the BIS and IOSCO is a significant step in cementing international co-operation over the regulation of banking activities. But it will not all be smooth sailing. National regulators have differing objectives and achieving consensus may be more of a problem than some observers imagine. That the will to achieve an element of communality exists is positive enough, but formulating standards which can apply around the world will be a formidable task. The Derivatives Policy Group's recommendations on management controls, published in March 1995, are reproduced in Appendix III to this book.

ASIAN OPPORTUNITIES

One of the biggest problems exists in the Pacific Rim, where Japanese agencies want more stringent controls while at the same time US and UK regulators favour a lighter touch. *The Economist* anticipates that Japanese banks will become bigger players in derivatives markets as domestic controls, which impede international capital flows, are relaxed. According to the Futures Industry Association in Washington, in 1994 the Tokyo International Financial Futures Exchange (TIFFE) was the second-fastest-growing exchange in the world. Comparing January to September figures for 1993 and 1994, TIFFE's futures and options contract volumes increased by 77 per cent to almost 30 million. In June 1994 alone volumes at TIFFE reached 4 million. 'In the third world, the dynamic Asian economies will make some leaps forward. Fund managers will see increasing scope for hedging securities position', commented *The Economist*.

The fastest-moving exchange is at São Paolo in Brazil, where contract volumes have increased by over 100 per cent. The Bolsa Mercadorias & de Futuros (BM&F) was opened in 1986 but its rapid expansion has been over the last few years, In 1993 contracts stood at 52 million, in 1994 they rose to 110 million. Financial volumes approached $800 billion. It has achieved this growth with one hand tied behind its back: the Brazilian economy has been anything but stable. And restrictions on foreign investment and trading links with exchanges abroad are compounded by poor liquidity in key products and a narrow customer base.

The Brazilian market for OTC derivatives is comparatively small at 10–15 per cent of exchange activity. Brazil's president, Fernando Henrique Cardoso, despite his recent election, has initiated economic reform on a grand scale to promote long-term stability in the economy. Analysts believe that this will be good for the derivatives market and will allow greater broadening of activities which had been limited by government policy. The BM&F wants greater liberalisation of policy to encourage greater foreign investment and to give it the opportunity to attempt to capture the business in futures on certain domestic agricultural commodities. At present, for example, Chicago has the lion's share of futures business on the Brazilian coffee market.

EUROPEAN EXPANSION

Provided that the Brazilian government is successful, BM&F is destined for a rosy future. The proliferation of exchanges in Europe creates different demands. Management at the Frankfurt futures exchange is worried about the growing number of exchanges in Europe. In 1994 volumes on the three leading European exchanges increased by 50 per cent over 1993. A decade ago the London International Financial Futures and Options Exchange (LIFFE) was the 'new kid on the block' while the United States accounted for 95 per cent of all trades. Today London achieves volumes which reach two-thirds of those in each of the Chicago exchanges (CBOT, CBOE and CME)

LIFFE plans to expand internationally – across the world – in after-hours trading with the world's largest trader, the Chicago Board of Trade, and the Sydney Futures Exchange.

(As a necessary caveat, however, it is important to mention that this proposal is at an early stage and its outcome is difficult to predict with certainty.) Matif, in Paris, which in 1994 recorded a 29 per cent growth in contract volumes, sees its future in extended links with smaller but rapidly growing futures exchanges in the Netherlands, Spain and Switzerland. The concept is fine but it will prove difficult to overcome the considerable differences which separate countries. Matif's cross-exchange futures co-operation with the Deutsche Terminbörse (DTB) in Frankfurt brings together two solid businesses. Matif's liquid contracts and DTB's superb technology could forge a formidable alliance.

THE TECHNOLOGY DILEMMA

One of the principal driving factors in the development of derivatives has been the growth in technology. Without the acceleration in technological systems the derivatives business simply could not have grown as fast as it has. In addition, the technology required for the advanced derivatives products has substantially enhanced systems for the whole financial sector.

Banks and other derivatives traders encounter the same problems in gathering data and no institution can cope with the speed and volumes of data needed to manage risk effectively. Laurie Morse in the *Financial Times* pointed to some of the difficulties in grappling with new systems:

> Reuter's costly experiment,with a global trading network, GLOBEX, has demonstrated that day-to-day demand for after hours access to financial futures contracts is meagre. However, such systems are invaluable because they provide escape routes during times of crisis.
>
> Futures industry experts say that just knowing that contracts can be exited after regular business hours significantly reduces market, credit and political risk. Grand visions for GLOBEX have

fizzled out with only the Chicago Mercantile Exchange and France's Matif still contributing to the system.

Links between exchanges allow them to trade in different time zones, in two product areas – government bond futures and energy derivatives – in particular. The planned association between CBOT, LIFFE and the Sydney Futures Exchange, mentioned earlier, will focus on government securities. Sydney is already operating an agreement with the New York Mercantile Exchange to list the Australian exchange's energy products on Nymex's after-hours computerised trading system Access.

At the micro rather than the macro level, the latest developments suggest that the use of bolt-on systems related to computer-aided design systems will increase. The graphics-based technology allows traders to create three-dimensional models which are particularly suitable for derivatives. This is because there are several related values to be drawn into a derivatives equation. Dealers believe that graphics technology will allow them to present a sketch (as it were) of their derivatives instruments. The hardware for the new graphics-related software will be the industry standard – UNIX. Regarded by many as a bizarre choice when it was first selected, UNIX gives end-users a choice of manufacturers and the capacity to change or extend hardware without altering the software. Users can share data while enjoying high processing power at local workstations.

The G30 study group recognised that there were significant steps to be taken before dealers achieved the degree of technological integration and sophistication which would lead to efficient risk management. Its recommendations included:

> dealers and end-users must ensure that adequate systems for data capture, processing, settlement and management reporting are in place so that derivatives transactions are conducted in an orderly and efficient manner in compliance with management policies. Dealers should have risk management systems that measure the

> risks incurred in their derivatives activities including market and credit risks. End-users should have risk management systems that measure the risks incurred in their derivatives activities based upon their nature, size and complexity.

At the time that the G30 conducted its study in 1993 some 40 per cent of confirmations were automated, 10 per cent partly automated, 45 per cent manual and 5 per cent of respondents did not know. Eighty per cent of dealers planned to automate their confirmations completely. The G30 study group reported that dealers who had integrated their front and back offices achieved enhanced operating efficiencies.

It seems likely that the demands of regulators will persuade traders and end-users to enhance their technology systems. To comply with the new standards, both will be obliged to introduce far more sophisticated and wide-ranging systems. In June 1994 William McDonough, president of the Federal Reserve Bank of New York, commented: 'the challenge of putting in place a state-of-the-art risk management information system is substantial, especially the commitment of dollars and human resources to install a sophisticated information system. In practical terms the banks may believe that they have sufficient vehicles in place but they do not have the total view.'

A leading consultant, Nigel Webb, head of risk management and derivatives at Terence Chapman Associates, was concerned when he spoke to the *Banker* in November 1994: 'The banks have come to a silly situation where each of the packages bought for each of the desks can do a certain amount of risk management. But there is no way of seeing the global consolidated picture of the risk – you may be horrendously exposed even though desks appear to be squared off.'

The Europeans who are also key players in the global derivatives markets have so far failed to match the drive and innovation of their US competitors. The latter have benefited from tighter regulatory control on risk management and they were able to start planning their strategy in this area early on. Bankers Trust began to develop its approach in 1988 and Citibank in 1990. But they have arrived at their strategy from distinctly different perspectives.

The Europeans . . . have so far failed to match the drive and innovation of their US competitors

Bankers Trust wanted to co-ordinate centrally with a sole hardware supplier and adopt a single-software approach. Conversely, Citibank's strategy is decentralised and localised. Its priority was open systems linked together and it claims that it has moved rapidly towards a fully integrated risk-management system. Key to its approach has been object-orientated techniques, which allow regional objectives to be smoothly installed. The whole strategy will last six years from its outset in 1991. According to Citibank's head of derivatives (Europe), Michael Hawker, integrated systems for derivatives will be in use globally by 1997.

The reason it is taking banks as long as this to install the most appropriate systems is the massive processing power required to handle the volume of trades in each twenty-four-hour cycle and the management of huge numbers of requests in a timely and effective manner. Nigel Webb told the *Banker* that achieving 90 per cent of performance effectiveness was a manageable task 'But to get that extra five per cent the [exponential] curve disappears off the graph.'

END-USER GROWTH

One of the most important derivatives industry trends of the 1990s has been growth in the numbers, types and range of end-users. Although they still have appreciable knowledge gaps about the products, how they work and their implications, the end-users have become more sophisticated. Despite the unflattering and highly critical publicity that derivatives have received, the satisfied customers significantly outweigh the unhappy or litigious ones. Phil Rivett of Coopers & Lybrand commented: 'What we're observing now is a wake up call for the end user community. It has pointed out to them some of the risks inherent in these types of products and it has given them cause to reassess the quality of their frameworks for identifying, assessing and managing risk.' This view was endorsed in November 1994 by Jean-Christian Cheysson, managing director of Credit Suisse Financial Products: 'Boards have not always been aware of the magnitude of the risks they have been running. A long stretch of successes made them sloppy.'

Through this process of reassessment corporate users have pulled out of the more complex and exotic derivatives and tend to favour the simpler and easier contracts which can be managed with greater certainty. Typical is McDonald's, the international fast-food restaurant chain. It has huge exposures to currency risk and continues to use derivatives in the way that it always has – prudently. Chuck Eberling, a spokesman for the company, told the *Financial Times*: 'We have always been conservative about derivatives.' The products are used only for basic financing. Phil Rivett argued that in 1994 companies had learned a single important lesson about derivatives – senior managers and directors need to be better informed about derivatives and their risks:

> There has been a general acknowledgement that corporate policies need to be better defined and a clearer statement of goals, objectives and risk tolerance by senior management and board directors. Also, companies are using instruments with multiple levels of risk. They have realised that they need appropriate models for evaluating such risks.

Among the packages available is a new 'black box' created by top derivatives bank JP Morgan – RiskMetrics. In November 1994 it was reviewed by the *Banker* in a feature entitled 'Tricks of the trade':

> A new box of tricks – RiskMetrics – has been opened by JP Morgan to banks, institutional investors and corporations. The service includes:
>
> - a written-up methodology on how to measure and implement value at risk;
> - historical volatility and correlation data on bond, currency and equities markets;
> - a system to calculate and analyse value at risk which will be provided by any of the nine vendors (Algorithmics, Barra International, Cats Software, Dow Jones Telerate, FEA, Price Waterhouse, Quantec, Sailfish Systems and Wall Street Systems) with which JP Morgan has teamed up.
>
> The smaller banks which use JP Morgan as a means of entering the derivatives market will be looking to see how comfortable they feel with the way the bank treats risk. The corporate treasurers, existing and potential customers of the bank, will be interested in seeing the bank placing itself as expert in this area. The third group interested in the service consists of all those who want to see what is new and different in the risk-management toolbox.
>
> If Morgan has something to add it may be an indication of where the bank anticipates the regulators (G30, BIS) are going with regard to risk management. Therefore, it may not be a coincidence that the head of the G30, Dennis Weatherstone, is also chairman of JP Morgan.
>
> Why is the company releasing its product free of charge? JP Morgan is hoping everyone can benefit from a greater understanding of how risk should be managed. Jacques Longerstacy, head of the market risk research unit that built RiskMetrics, says another goal is 'to provide a common measurement framework that people could be using through the industry. The only way to achieve that is if you make it publicly available.' He adds: 'If you charge for the

product you are never going to get it to be used as a widely available benchmark. The overall impact on the business of the bank and the potential relationships that we have with our clients far outweigh the cost of developing and managing RiskMetrics.'

The cynics claim that the announcement is a subtle ploy to raise JP Morgan's business in the derivatives market. 'One way of upstaging the competition is to be shown to be very well up on risk management,' says one city insider.

He continues: 'The timing for the announcement could not be better.' The investment bank is in the process of re-engineering its swaps business worldwide, moving from basic or standard products into more heavily engineered customised swaps. 'If JP Morgan can be shown to have a pretty rigorous way of dealing with risk management then it will be winning much business.' . . .

If anyone is thinking of releasing a similar product they will also have to give it away free of charge.

NEW PRODUCTS

The fall in the dollar and world bond markets triggered the spate of corporate losses in 1994 and particularly hit highly leveraged holders of OTC products such as structured notes. The ensuing upsets also took their toll on equity markets and commodity prices, shaking up the delicate projections of dealers and end-users.

Nevertheless, the growth in derivatives products continues but perhaps with a more qualitative dimension to product selection. The level of increase from 1992 to 1993 showed that the notional value of swaps and other OTC products had risen by 58.5 per cent to $8,475 billion. Few anticipate anything like such a good year when the 1994 figures are published. Interest rate swaps are now a commonplace and effective risk-management tool and, by the standards of some derivatives products, they are relatively reliable.

Exchange-traded swaps have the advantage of being easily

switched from one market to another in a matter of moments but sometimes these do not always meet the precise needs of end-users; hence the growth in the OTC trade.

The collapse of international barriers and the introduction of global technology systems have fuelled the continuing growth of swaps and the international aspect of this market will expand. Stephen Compton, head of interest rate derivatives trading at Citibank in London, said: 'the large corporates are now using swaps in a far more sophisticated way and exploiting their full potential'.

Although equity derivatives were partly blamed for the crash of 1987, they have remained comparatively unscathed by recent market problems. In London alone, equity futures contracts increased from 458,000 in 1987 to 4.3 million in 1994. The United Kingdom is ahead of the rest of Europe, but in the United States the turnover in equities futures is ten times that of the cash market.

OTC commodity swaps increased substantially in 1994, caused by extensive price rises in a range of raw materials. The exchange-traded market has been strong for some considerable time but investors have been attracted by the flexibility and variety of instruments of OTC products. Around 90 per cent of the world's fifteen largest commodity producers use swaps to hedge price risk, But investors have also become increasingly attracted to the commodity-based derivatives to exploit gains. This increased interest has prompted big derivatives banks like JP Morgan, Goldman Sachs and Merrill Lynch to offer a variety of instruments pegged to commodity baskets and indices. Commodity-based investment funds are also a recent creation. A BZW commodities trust will attempt to outperform the Goldman Sachs commodities index.

There will also be an emphasis on the more exotic products which have characterised the history of derivatives trading.

Hedge funds which have taken a hammering in 1994 may surmount their difficulties. Tass, a London research firm, said that $75 to $80 billion is invested in around 850 hedge funds worldwide. These funds reported outstanding results in 1993 but, linked to the bond market, saw their fortunes reverse in February 1994 when the US Federal Reserve raised short-term interest rates and the bond market collapsed. Protagonists point to past performance and the increasing sophistication of market information in arguing that investors should stay calm. At the moment an act of faith appears to be required but that may be true of all investments at some stage in their cycle.

There will also be an emphasis on the more exotic products

On the farther horizon, the 'rocket scientists' are preparing to take the concept of derivatives still further. US banks are focusing on new products to manage credit risk, which they estimate will be a market potentially worth $1,000 billion. Among them are Credit Suisse First Boston, Merrill Lynch and Bankers Trust. Another kind of derivative will concentrate on market forces which influence the allocation of scarce resources: for example, secondary markets in trading pollution allowances issued after the introduction of the US Clean Air Act. Nymex in New York, which is the world's leading energy exchange, proposes to introduce electricity futures in 1995.

Learning points

1 Two key issues have emerged from the industry's Group of 30 latest (1994) survey on the derivatives trading and user sector:
(a) better risk-management systems are still needed;
(b) the level of education must be improved.

2 Banks and trading houses generally have better risk-management systems than have corporate treasuries.

3 Significant improvement has taken place since the last G30 report and survey, in 1993.

4 Some regulation may be imposed to establish risk-management requirements and perhaps limitations on organisations which may be traded with.

5 Considerable work on policies and systems still needs to be done within corporate end-users.

10

GLOSSARY

Derivatives and risk-management tools generally utilise a range of terms which non-specialists can find baffling and sometimes amusing. Dealers have a preference for dramatic, colourful and exotic language. In this chapter the reader will find strangles, underwater swaps, naked options, cocktail swaps, deep in the money, voluntary termination and butterfly spreads. Apart from their theatrical and sometimes lyrical names, these terms are principally descriptions of precise techniques and activities which give form to derivatives trading. Without an appreciation of these fundamentals of the sector, it is impossible to gain an effective understanding of the day-to-day management of derivatives.

In this summary of the typical terminology of the sector I have included some terms which may already be familiar to readers with an appreciation of the capital markets – but they are here because they help to give a more complete picture. The definitions inevitably use some jargon but I have attempted to explain th[illegible] simple English.

Absolute rate: this term is commonly used in the Eur[illegible] refers to a bid or offer made on Euronotes (shor[illegible] up promissory notes) which is not expressed [illegible] particular funding base such as LIBOR or Treas[illegible]

American option: an option which can be exercise[illegible] before its expiry date.

Amount: this expression may appear self-explanatory bu[illegible] terminology can often reflect a meaning which is peculiar to this industry alone. In this case 'amount' refers to a quantity which a person wishes to sell against US dollars.

Arbitrage: possibly the single most famous term from Wall Street in the 1980s. It conveys all the glamour and excitement of America's most fashionable industry of the decade. The term also became a byword for the more notorious practices in the sector.

In precise terms, it means the purchase or sale of any financial instrument in one market and the almost simultaneous sale or purchase in another centre. The aim is to exploit – for financial gain – differences in exchange rates. It can lead to spectacular gains or create horrendous losses. Arbitrage requires great skill and a lot of luck. The term may also involve borrowing funds in one centre and their conversion or use in another centre.

Asset: in relation to foreign exchange markets, this is the right to receive from a counterparty an amount of currency either in respect of a balance sheet asset, for example a loan, or at a specified date in the future in respect of an unmatched forward or spot deal.

Asset allocation: the process by which a manager divides investment funds between different asset classes to provide diversification and/or the highest return.

Asset-based swap: an asset-based swap links a fixed-rate bond with a swap from an investment banker. The arrangement allows the purchaser to buy floating-rate paper from an issuer who would not normally enter a floating-rate market – or fixed-rate paper from an issuer who would not normally enter a fixed-rate market.

Assignment: the sale of a swap contract by one of the parties to someone who is not a party. This usually involves a lump sum payment. Swap assignments are difficult because they require the approval of the other original party.

At a premium: currency which is more expensive to purchase forward than it is for spot delivery.

At the money: an option where the strike price equals the current spot price.

Average rate option: this is also known as an Asian option. It occurs when the settlement for a particular deal is fixed between the strike price and the current average prices of the underlying asset or the index on given dates.

Barrier options: there is a whole range of barrier options. They depend for their payoff and survival on achieving specific objectives based on the price performance of the underlying. If the underlying achieves or goes through a predetermined price level at any time during the life of the option, the deal will be valid or not as the case may be. These are termed 'path-dependent' options. Among them are:

- *Down-and-out call/put* – an option which becomes valueless if it falls below a predetermined price.
- *Down-and-in call/put* – the opposite of the above. If the market price of the underlying security drops below the predetermined price, the option becomes effective.
- *Up-and-out call/put* – an option which becomes worthless if the price of the underlying rises above a pre-agreed level.
- *Up-and-in call/put* – the option becomes valid if the price of the underlying exceeds the agreed level.

Base currency: the currency in which the operating results of a bank are reported.

Basis: the difference between the current spot price of an item and its futures contract price.

Basis convergence: the process where the futures price of a contract approaches its market spot price as the delivery date nears.

Basis point: 1/100 of one percentage point.

Bear spread: a spread involves put or call options on the same underlying but with different expiry dates or strike prices. There are three common spreads: bear, bull and butterfly. These are strategies or market approaches. A bear spread operates when the option has a higher strike price than the average. In these circumstances, the manager would sell a call and buy another at a higher price or sell a put and buy another put at a higher price (see chapter 6, on options).

Bid: the price at which a party is prepared to buy. When agreed, the bid has been hit.

Box options: this allows the manager to use a tax-positive technique to create capital gains while adopting a conservative approach to investment. Equity options are bought. The capital gains from their payoffs are then offset against current capital losses. If the procedure generates a loss there is no exposure.

Broken dates: deals not for spot or fixed rates, sometimes called odd dates.

Bull spread: See **bear spread**. The same principle applies save that this refers to a situation where the option has a lower strike price than average. The strategy is to buy a call and sell a call at a higher price or buy a put and sell a put at a higher price.

Butterfly spread: See **bear spread** and **bull spread**. Two options in the middle – with regard to strike price – written against one option on either side but all on the same instrument. The strategy is complicated and is described in chapter 6 on options.

Buy-back valuation: a specific type of valuation of a forward exchange deal. The current exchange rate is applied to the remaining period of a particular transaction.

Cable: the spot dollar/sterling rate.

Call: the right to acquire an underlying instrument at a predetermined price and date in the future. Also known as a call option. The right to buy is the 'call'.

Callable swap: here a swap is used together with callable bond issues. A bond issuer is paid a premium by the party who has a right to call the swap.

Cap: this is a contract between a borrower or a lender where the borrower will not have to pay more than an agreed maximum interest rate on borrowed funds.

Carry: the return on a trader's book net of financing cost. The return can be positive or negative.

Cheapest to deliver: the cheapest instrument that will allow a futures contract to be delivered. This is available when the contract requirements can be satisfied by more than one type of instrument.

Choice: a principal as a buyer or seller at one price.

Clearing house: an institute linked to a futures or options exchange which matches and guarantees trades and holds performance bonds posted by a dealer. Acts as a counterparty to every trade to reduce credit risk.

Closed position: a matched or balanced position in a currency where total assets and liabilities in that currency are equal.

Cocktail swap: this is a currency swap which involves a number of different swap transactions.

Collar: a floating-rate debt contract which defines the highest and lowest interest rates to be paid by the borrower.

Combination: a combination unites calls and puts on the same underlying, so that they are both bought or both written.

Commodity swap: a swap where counterparties exchange cash flows. This is based on a commodity price on at least one side of the transaction (see chapter 5).

Compound option: a kind of super-option. The holder has an option on an option, the right to buy on a pre-set date for a pre-agreed premium.

Confirmation: written agreement to a transaction, exchanged by both parties.

Conversion: an asset or liability in one currency is exchanged for a similar asset or liability in another currency.

Conversion account: for the tidy-minded. It is the ledger account representing an uncovered position in a currency; sometimes called position accounts.

Convertibility: self-explanatory – facility to convert one currency into another.

Counterparty: the other party in a deal.

Covered call: a call, exercised by the holder, on the asset/security underlying the option.

Covered put option: writing a put option on which the writer has a short position.

Cross deal: a foreign exchange deal involving two currencies, neither of which is the base currency of a dealing bank. Also used to describe a deal not involving US dollars.

Cross rate: exchange rate used for two currencies neither of which is the base currency of a dealing bank. Also a rate between two currencies other than the US dollar.

Currency swap: a deal where two parties exchange designated amounts – or loans – in specified but different currencies at the outset. They also exchange interest rate payments in the currencies over the term of a swap and re-exchange principal at maturity.

Custom option: another term for a customised or over-the-counter (OTC) option.

Daily limit: limit imposed by futures exchanges on the maximum price variation in one day.

Deal date: the day a deal or contract is entered into.

Dealing slip/dealing ticket: the base document on which a dealer records all the details of a particular deal.

Deep in the money: this indicates that an option has strong intrinsic value. For a put, the strike price substantially exceeds the spot price for the underlying. If a call, the spot price significantly exceeds the strike price.

Deferred strike: also called 'deferred start option' or 'forward start option'. The holder is empowered to defer setting the strike price until a future date agreed by both parties.

Delayed swap: a swap which does not start immediately.

Delta hedging: a method of hedging options. The price or value of an option will move by an amount equal to a movement in the price of delta multiplied by the quantity of the underlying. So the writer of an option can protect the investment from price movements on the option by holding an amount – delta – of the underlying.

Deposit swap: a series of transactions where a deposit is accepted in one currency, and the proceeds are sold into a second currency and lent on. Sometimes called a 'switch' or 'covered interest arbitrage'.

Details: information needed by a dealer after completion of a transaction, i.e. names, rate and dates.

Dollar payer: institution that pays US dollars in a currency swap.

ECU: European Currency Unit. A standard unit of measurement based on a basket of European currencies.

Effective date: the date on which fixed and floating interest starts accruing.

End/end: forward swaps or currency deposits which start before or at spot delivery on the last working day of the month, and mature on the last working day of a subsequent month.

End-user: a counterparty which uses a derivatives solution to limit exposure. End-users may include non-financial corporations or governments.

Equity swap: a contract between two counterparties to exchange two different cash flows over time. Over the life of a swap one party agrees to pay the rate of return based on an equity or equity index while the other party agrees to pay a floating or fixed rate of interest.

Euro commercial paper: a generic term for the market in non-underwritten Euronotes. Commercial paper is normally issued on a continuous basis by one or more dealers.

Eurocurrency: a freely convertible currency held outside the domestic country of that currency. The main currency traded is US dollars, hence Eurodollars.

European option: an option which can be exercised only on the expiry date.

Exchange-traded options: options whose terms are standardised and traded on recognised exchanges. These include the Chicago Board Options Exchange, the New York Futures Exchange and LIFFE in London.

Exercise period: the time during which an option can be exercised.

Exercise rate: also called the strike price. The rate at which a holder may exercise its option during the life of a contract.

Expiry date: the last day of the life of an option contract.

Exploding option: also called a 'one-touch option'. A European-style call spread with an early exercise price trigger.

Extendable swap: a swap which allows one of the parties to extend the transaction.

Firm: a dealer making a bid or offer on a 'firm' basis. Best practice is to say how firm is 'firm', e.g. 'firm for one minute' or 'firm for one million dollars'.

Fixed-rate payer: party who makes the fixed-rate payment in a swap (also known as a fixed-rate coupon) to the floating-rate payer.

Floating-rate payer: the opposite of **fixed-rate payer,** also known as the variable-rate payer.

Floor: the minimum interest rate for the borrower in a floating-rate debt contract.

Foreign currency payer: the non-US currency payer in a currency swap. Referred to by the currency involved, e.g. the sterling payer.

Forward: an OTC agreement for buyer and seller to exchange a specified good at a particular price on a given date.

Forward deal: a deal with a value date longer than a spot deal.

Forward/forward: a forward sale against a forward purchase or vice versa.

Forward rate: the price of currency which matures beyond the spot date.

Futures Commission Merchant (FCM): a broker registered with the Commodity Futures Trading Commission who conducts trades on a futures exchange for customers.

Futures contract: an exchange-traded contract for the future delivery of a standardised quantity of an item. Changes in the market value of a futures contract can be settled daily.

Gap: a mismatch between maturities. In practice, gap exposure is interest rate exposure.

General ledger multicurrency system: a bookkeeping system which includes the maintenance of a general ledger for each currency, the link between currency general ledgers and the base currency general ledger by means of conversion accounts.

Hedge: a technique for reducing the risk of an underlying by using an appropriate derivative. Usually limits the potential benefit of the underlying position. Also generic term for limiting or containing risk.

Hedged swap: a swap with no underlying asset or obligation but for which interest rate risk is reduced or eliminated in some other way.

Holder: the holder of a contract. The holder has the right to exercise a contract against the writer.

Hybrid security: a complex security which can integrate any combination of two or more risk-management building blocks.

In the money: a product which has intrinsic value. For example, a call option whose exercise price is lower, or a put option whose exercise price is higher, than the market price of the underlying instrument.

Initial margin: a deposit in cash left with the broker to open a futures contract. The amount varies according to whether the contract is a hedge or a speculation, depending on the rules of the exchange.

Interest-rate swap: exchange between parties of fixed- and floating-rate debt in a particular currency where the rate is predetermined. There are three main types:

- *coupon swaps* (fixed rate to floating rate in the same currency);
- *basis swaps* (one floating-rate index to another floating-rate index in the same currency);
- *cross-currency interest rate swaps* (fixed rate in one currency to floating rate in another).

Intermediary: a counterparty who enters into a deal to earn fees or trading profits. Many intermediaries are US money-center banks, major US and UK investment and merchant banks and major Japanese securities companies.

Intrinsic value: difference between the strike price of a product and the spot price of the underlying item, but never less than zero.

ISDA: International Swaps and Derivatives Association.

Ladder: also 'step-lock option'. It provides the holder of an option with a mechanism to lock in gains from an underlying security during the life of an option.

Liability: in the area of foreign exchange, the obligation to deliver to a counterparty an amount of currency either in respect of a balance sheet holding (e.g. a deposit) at a specified future date or in respect of an unmatured forward or spot sale.

LIBID: the London Interbank Bid Rate. The rate at which a bank is willing to pay for funds in the international interbank market.

LIBOR: London Interbank Offered Rate. The rate at which banks offer to lend funds in the international interbank market.

LIMEAN: the mean of LIBID and LIBOR.

Limited partnership: more common in the United States than in Europe. This is an instrument where an investor becomes a partner in a fund to benefit directly from the fund's profits (or, of course, share in its losses).

Locked: either way (same) price (or yield) from a broker or dealer at which he will buy or sell a security.

Long: excess of purchases over sales.

Long future: a futures contract to purchase an item – a long position.

Long option: a purchased option with a call or a put on the underlying asset.

Lookback option: not an opportunity for incompetent derivatives salesmen to put right their mistakes but another package for draftsmen who think in algebraic formulae. The payout on this type of option is calculated using the highest intrinsic value of the underlying security or index during the life of the option. In the case of a lookback call the highest market price is used; in the case of a lookback put the lowest market price.

Maintenance margin: the level to which a margin account may fall before the holder must bring the balance up to the initial minimum level. Also called 'variation margin'.

Margin: the stated margin (spread) is expressed as a percentage, added to or subtracted from a reference interest rate (e.g. LIBOR) to establish the coupon of a floating-rate instrument.

Mark to market: Process of valuing a derivatives transaction by reference to the current market value of the underlying.

Market going better (or up): a term from the bond markets when prices are rising and interest rates are falling.

Market going worse (or down): prices falling and interest rates rising in the bond markets.

Matched book of swaps: a strategy used by an intermediary in an effort to minimise interest rate risk by holding offsetting swap positions with a range of counterparties.

Matched swap: a swap where the underlying has interest payment terms similar to the swap itself.

Matching: the process of ensuring that purchases and sales in each currency and deposits given and taken in each currency are matched, by amount and maturity. A bank may regard itself as matched for all practical purposes when the amounts are matched, even when there is some mismatching of maturities.

Maturity date: same as value date. The settlement date on which the exchange of currencies between the parties will take place.

Middle rate: median between bid and offer.

Mine: a dealer states that the spot or forward (whichever has been quoted by a counterparty) which is taken is definitely *his*. The amount *must be clearly stated.*

Minimum rate: for floating-rate paper, the interest rate below which the coupon may not be fixed.

Mirror swap: a reverse swap written with the original counterparty.

Multiple-option: a group of two or more options with different terms, held as a single investment or hedging strategy.

Naked call option: a call option where the writer does not currently own the underlying that would be delivered if the option were exercised.

Naked dogs: dogs are 'emerging market' currencies – those which are difficult to convert – taken collectively as a basket. The basket is made up of a selection of bonds issued in exchange for the rescheduled debt of developing countries (Brady bonds). The dogs are termed 'naked' because the yield on the US long bond, which in its zero-rated coupon form is used as collateral for these issues, is taken out of the return on the Bradies.

Naked option: generic term for the **naked call option** and **naked put option**.

Naked put option: a put option where the writer does not currently have a short position in the commodity underlying the option.

Nostro account: a foreign currency account kept at another bank, usually but not necessarily a foreign correspondent bank.

Notional principal: a hypothetical amount on which swap payments are based. The notional principal in an interest rate swap is never paid or received by the parties to the swap.

Offer: the price at which one is prepared to sell.

Offer rate: the fixed rate a financial institution is willing to receive in a swap.

Offsetting swap position: two swaps which counterbalance each other to reduce interest rate risk.

On-the-run: the most recently issued three-, six- or twelve-month Treasury bills.

Open position: difference between current and future contracted assets and liabilities in a particular currency. Can be measured either as an individual currency position or covering all foreign currencies.

Option: a contract to give the owner the right – not the obligation – to buy (call) or sell (put) a specified quantity of a specific instrument or commodity at a fixed price at any time on or before a given date (American-style) or on a given date (European-style).

Option value/option premium: the value of an option at any given time.

OTC options: over-the-counter options.

Out of the money: a call option whose exercise price is greater, or a put option whose exercise price is less, than the market price of the underlying instrument.

Outperformance option: a call option which allows an investor to capitalise on diverging performances of two underlying securities, which can be individual stocks, customised baskets of stocks or a specified index.

Over borrowed fixed: counterparty pays fixed and receives floating rate.

Over lent fixed: counterparty pays floating and receives fixed rate.

Paper: generic term for securities.

Par: the price is the same on both sides of the swap.

Parity: the premium on an option is exactly equal to its intrinsic value.

Pay-up: additional cash outlay on the sale of one block of securities and purchase of another.

Pick-up: a gain from selling one block of securities and buying another.

Pip: also 'point' – a 100th part of a cent in price. Movements in exchange rates are often expressed in points/pips. For example, a fall from £1 = $1.8535 to £1 = $1.8533 is a movement of two pips.

Plain vanilla swap: a US dollar interest rate swap. One party makes floating-rate payments based on six-month LIBOR rates and receives fixed-rate funds. These are quoted as a spread over the rate of the on-the-run US Treasury securities. Maturity is usually fixed at five to seven years and deal size is normally at least $50–100 million.

Position: the netted total commitments in a given currency or interest rate. A position can be:

- *flat or square* – no exposure;
- *long* – overbought;
- *short* – oversold.

Position clerk: a clerk who assists the dealer and ensures that completed deal tickets are filed promptly with the accounts department.

Premium: amount paid by a buyer to the seller for the option right. The premium is expressed in various ways: for example, as a percentage per unit of the underlying instrument, or as a number of cents per unit in the underlying instrument.

Put: the right to sell the underlying instrument at a predetermined date and price in the future.

Quanto option: an option where foreign exchange risks have been eliminated. Also called a guaranteed exchange rate option or currency protected option.

Quote: a price given as an indication rather than a firm commitment. Usually one is not prepared to move on the price.

Reverse swap: this offsets the interest rate or currency exposure on an existing swap. Reverse swaps are designed to realise capital gains.

Risk reversal: combines the purchase of a put option with the sale of a call option. The put option preserves the capital value of the holding while the sale of the call option reduces or eliminates the cost of this insurance. The penalty is giving up some of the positive potential of the stock.

Rocket scientist: individual responsible for fashioning derivatives products. Refers to the complex nature of derivatives.

Round turn: the opening and subsequent closing of a futures position. Fees for futures contracts are usually on the basis of a round turn.

Same day transaction: a transaction that will mature on the same day as the contract is made.

Settlement: there are various forms of settlement arrangements. Some are listed below:

- *Cash settlement* – delivery of securities against payment where the settlement date is the same as the trade date. This term used by the money markets in the United States. In the United Kingdom it is known, alternatively, as same-day settlement.

- *Regular way settlement* – trades in which settlement occurs on the next business day after the trade day.
- *Skip day settlement* – settlement on the second business day after the trade day. Usage of this term is confined to the US domestic market; in the UK foreign exchange markets it is known as spot settlement.
- *Corporate settlement* – settlement five business days after the trade date (in the United States) but after one week in Eurobond trading.

Short: oversold.

Short future: a futures contract to sell an item – a short position.

Short option: a written option.

Spot: foreign exchange transactions for which the value date is two business days from the date the transaction is undertaken.

Spot price: the exchange rate for settlement two working days ahead.

Spread: combines call and put options on the same underlying instrument but with different expiry dates or strike prices; some are bought and some written.

Square: purchases and sales are equal.

Straddle: dealers like straddling. This popular technique is widely used and combines a call and a put on the same underlying at the same strike and with the same expiry date.

Strangle: another dramatic term. Similar to a straddle except that the calls and puts are bought at different prices.

Strike price: the price specified in an option contract at which the buyer can purchase (in the case of a call) or sell (in the case of a put) the item underlying the option.

Subject: there are two common uses of the term 'subject':

- *subject bid or offer* – price subject to purchaser's approval of names dependent on credit limits;
- *bid or offer subject* – indication of a price a purchaser is willing to pay but which may not be firm.

Swap: the simultaneous purchase and sale of the same amount of a given currency for two different dates against the sale and purchase of another. A swap can be spot against forward or forward against forward. In essence swapping is somewhat similar to borrowing one currency and lending another for the same period. However, any rate of return or cost of funds is expressed in the price differential between the two sides of the transaction.

Swap price: a price stated as a differential between two dates. When the buying price is cheaper than the selling price it is called 'earning the points' or dealing in one's favour. When the opposite occurs this is termed 'paying the points' or dealing against oneself.

Swaption: an option to enter a swap contract.

SWIFT: Society for Worldwide Interbank Financial Telecommunications. A sophisticated computerised international communications system for the settlement of foreign currency payments between banks.

Swissy: the US dollar/Swiss franc rate.

Switch: alternative name for deposit swap.

Synthetic future: a linked option position equivalent to a position in a futures contract. It is created by buying a put and writing a call at the same strike price and with the same expiry date. This is equivalent to a short position in a futures contract. Alternatively, a call can be bought and a put written at the same strike price and with the same expiry date. This is the same as a long position in a futures contract.

Take-out: additional cash on the sale of one block of securities and the purchase of another. See **pay-up.**

Texas hedge: a technique which increases risk. Two or more related positions whose risk is cumulative rather than offsetting.

Three-month Canada cross: in the London dealing environment, the three-month forward cross rate between Canadian dollars and pounds sterling.

Tick: smallest fraction of price at which a security is typically traded.

Ticket: a dealing slip.

Time value: the difference between the market value of an option and its intrinsic value.

Traded option: an option traded publicly on an exchange.

Translation: accounting terminology for expressing one currency in relation to another.

Uncovered sale: sale of an option without a position in the underlying instrument.

Underlying: key component of a derivatives transaction; the asset which is tied to (and thus underlies) a second component (the derivative) to make up a deal.

Under reference: a deal cannot be finalised without reference to the principal who placed the order.

Underwater swap: unprofitable swap position (from the perspective of one counterparty) caused by adverse movement in interest rates. The losing counterparty makes net payments to the intermediary and would need to pay the other party to terminate the agreement.

Unmatched, naked or one-sided swap: a swap for which no underlying or liability exists.

Unwinding a swap: ending a swap agreement.

Valeur compensée: payments are valeur compensée when payment by one party in one centre and settlement by the other party in another centre take place on the same day.

Value date: settlement date on which the exchange of currencies between parties will take place.

Value at risk (VAR): a system of risk management for derivatives products and portfolios. It is based on statistics and is advanced by many banks as the fairest system.

Voluntary termination: cancellation of a swap contract which is agreed by both parties. Usually involves a lump sum payment from one party to the other.

Vostro account: a local currency current account kept with a bank by another bank. See **nostro account**.

Warrant: an option to purchase or sell an underlying instrument at a given price and time or series of prices and times. A warrant differs from a put or call option in that it is ordinarily issued for longer than a year.

When issued (WI): trades before issue, in which settlement occurs and if the Treasury or government agency issues the certificate, reflecting the period between the announcement of a security's auction and its issue.

Writer: the seller of the option. The writer must fulfil the obligation of the option contact should the holder choose to exercise the option.

Write/buy: a dealer is said to have written the option and an end-user is said to have bought the option.

Written account: either a put or a call option from the perspective of the party receiving the premium – the writer of the option.

Yours: opposite to **mine.**

Zero-coupon interest rate swap: a swap which enables a borrower to issue a zero-coupon bond and swap the interest for floating rate. The borrower pays floating rate and receives fixed. However, the fixed-rate payment is paid at the termination of the swap.

APPENDIX I

The Basle Committee/IOSCO risk-management guidelines

The risk-management process

1. The primary components of a sound risk-management process are the following: a comprehensive risk-measurement approach; a detailed structure of limits, guidelines and other parameters used to govern risk taking; and a strong management information system for controlling, monitoring and reporting risks. These components are fundamental to both derivatives and non-derivatives activities alike. Moreover, the underlying risks associated with these activities, such as credit, market, liquidity, operations and legal risk, are not new to banking, although their measurement and management can be more complex. Accordingly, the process of risk management for derivatives activities should be integrated into the institution's overall risk-management system to the fullest extent possible using a conceptual framework common to the institution's other activities. Such a common framework enables the institution to manage its risk exposure more effectively, especially since the various individual risks involved in derivatives activities can, at times, be interconnected and can often transcend specific markets.

2. As is the case with all risk-bearing activities, the risk exposures an institution assumes in its derivatives activities should be fully supported by an adequate capital position. The institution should ensure that its capital position is sufficiently strong to support all derivatives risks on a fully consolidated basis and that adequate capital is maintained in all group entities engaged in these activities.

Risk measurement

3. An institution's system for measuring the various risks of derivatives activities should be both comprehensive and accurate. Risk

should be measured and aggregated across trading and non-trading activities on an institution-wide basis to the fullest extent possible.

4. While the use of a single prescribed risk-measurement approach for management purposes may not be essential, the institution's procedures should enable management to assess exposures on a consolidated basis. Risk measures and the risk-measurement process should be sufficiently robust to reflect accurately the multiple types of risks facing the institution. Risk-measurement standards should be understood by relevant personnel at all levels of the institution – from individual traders to the board of directors – and should provide a common framework for limiting and monitoring risk-taking activities.

5. With regard to dealer operations, the process of marketing derivatives positions to market is fundamental to measuring and reporting exposures accurately and on a timely basis. An institution active in dealing foreign exchange, derivatives and other traded instruments should have the ability to monitor credit exposures, trading positions and market movements at least daily. Some institutions should also have the capacity, or at least the goal, of monitoring their more actively traded products on a real-time basis.

6. Analysing stress situations, including combinations of market events that could affect the banking organisation, is also an important aspect of risk measurement. Sound risk-measurement practices include identifying possible events or changes in market behaviour that could have unfavourable effects on the institution and assessing the ability of the institution to withstand them. These analyses should consider not only the likelihood of adverse events, reflecting their probability, but also 'worst case' scenarios. Ideally, such worst case analysis should be conducted on an institution-wide basis by taking into account the effect of unusual changes in prices or volatilities, market illiquidity or the default of a large counterparty across both the derivatives and cash trading portfolios and the loan and funding portfolios.

7. Such stress tests should not be limited to quantitative exercises that compute potential losses or gains. They should also include more qualitative analyses of the actions management might take under particular scenarios. Contingency plans outlining operating procedures and lines of communication, both formal and informal, are important products of such qualitative analyses.

Limiting risks

8. A sound system of integrated institution-wide limits and risk-taking guidelines is an essential component of the risk-management process. Such a system should set boundaries for organisational risk-taking and should also ensure that positions that exceed certain predetermined levels receive prompt management attention. The limit system should be consistent with the effectiveness of the organisation's overall risk-management process and with the adequacy of its capital position. An appropriate limit system should permit management to control exposures, to initiate discussion about opportunities and risks and to monitor actual risk-taking against predetermined tolerances, as determined by the board of directors and senior management.

9. Global limits should be set for each major type of risk involved in an institution's derivatives activities. These limits should be consistent with the institution's overall risk-measurement approach and should be integrated to the fullest extent possible with institution-wide limits on those risks as they arise in all other activities of the institution. Where appropriate, the limit system should provide the capability to allocate limits down to individual business units.

10. If limits are exceeded, such occurrences should be made known to senior management and approved only by authorised personnel. Those positions should also prompt discussions about the consolidated risk-taking activities of the institution or the unit conducting the derivatives activities. The seriousness of limit exceptions depends in large part upon management's approach toward setting limits and on the actual size of individual and organisational limits relative to the institution's capacity to take risk. An institution with relatively conservative limits may encounter more exceptions to those limits than an institution with less restrictive limits.

Reporting

11. An accurate, informative and timely management information system is essential to the prudent operation of derivatives activities. Accordingly, the quality of the management information system is an important factor in the overall effectiveness of the risk-management process. The risk-management function should monitor and report its

measures of risks to appropriate levels of senior management and to the board of directors. In dealer operations, exposures and profit and loss statements should be reported at least daily to managers who supervise but do not, themselves, conduct those activities. More frequent reports should be made as market conditions dictate. Reports to other levels of senior management and the board may occur less frequently, but the frequency of reporting should provide these individuals with adequate information to judge the changing nature of the institution's risk profile.

12. Management information systems should translate the measured risk for derivatives activities from a technical and quantitative format to one that can be easily read and understood by senior managers and directors, who may not have specialised and technical knowledge of derivatives products. Risk exposures arising from various derivatives products should be reported to senior managers and directors using a common conceptual framework for measuring and limiting risks.

Management evaluation and review

13. Management should ensure that the various components of the institution's risk-management process are regularly reviewed and evaluated. This review should take into account changes in the activities of the institution and in the market environment, since the changes may have created exposures that require additional attention. Any material changes to the risk-management system should also be reviewed.

14. The risk-management functions should regularly assess the methodologies, models and assumptions used to measure risk and limit exposures. Proper documentation of these elements of the risk-measurement system is essential for conducting meaningful reviews. The review of limit structures should compare limits to actual exposures and should also consider whether existing measures of exposure and limits are appropriate in view of the institution's past performance and current capital position.

15. The frequency and extent to which an institution should re-evaluate its risk-measurement methodologies and models depends, in part,

on the specific risk exposures created by their derivatives activities, on the pace and nature of market changes and on the pace of innovation with respect to measuring and managing risks. At a minimum, an institution with significant derivatives activities should review the underlying methodologies of its models at least annually – and more often as market conditions dictate – to ensure they are appropriate and consistent, such internal evaluations may, in many cases, be supplemented by reviews by external auditors or other qualified outside parties, such as consultants who have expertise with highly technical models and risk-management techniques. Assumptions should be evaluated on a continual basis.

16. The institution should also have an effective process to evaluate and review the risks involved in products that are either new to it, or new to the marketplace and of potential interest to the institution. It should also introduce new products in a manner that adequately limits potential losses and permits the testing of internal systems. An institution should not become involved in a product at significant levels until senior management and all relevant personnel (including those in risk management, internal control, legal, accounting and auditing) understand the product and are able to integrate the product into the institution's risk-measurement and control systems.

APPENDIX II

The Basle Committee/IOSCO risk-profile guidelines

Risk profiles

[*Paragraph 1 is not material for present purposes.*]

Credit risk (including settlement risk)

2. Broadly defined, credit risk is the risk that a counterparty will fail to perform on an obligation to the institution. The institution should evaluate both settlement and pre-settlement credit risk at the customer level across all products. On settlement day, the exposure to counterparty default may equal the full value of any cash flow or securities the institution is to receive. Prior to settlement, credit risk is measured as the sum of the replacement cost of the position, plus an estimate of the institution's potential future exposure from the instrument as a result of market changes. Replacement cost should be determined using current market prices or generally accepted approaches for estimating the present value of future payments required under each contract, given current market conditions.

3. Potential credit risk exposure is measured more subjectively than current exposure and is primarily a function of the time remaining to maturity and the expected volatility of the price, rate or index underlying the contract. Dealers and large derivatives participants should assess potential exposure through simulation analysis or other sophisticated techniques, which, when properly designed and implemented can produce estimates of potential exposure that incorporate both portfolio-specific characteristics and current market conditions. Smaller end-users may measure this exposure by using 'add-ons' based on more general characteristics. In either case, the assumptions underlying the institution's risk measure should be reasonable and if the institution measures exposure using a portfolio approach, it should do so in a prudent manner.

4. An institution may use master netting agreements and various credit enhancements, such as collateral or third-party guarantees, to reduce its counterparty credit risk. In such cases, an institution's credit exposures should reflect these risk-reducing features only to the extent that the agreements and recourse provisions are legally enforceable in all relevant jurisdictions. This legal enforceability should extend to any insolvency proceeding of the counterparty. The institution should be able to demonstrate that it has exercised due diligence in evaluating the enforceability of these contracts and that individual transactions have been executed in a manner that provides adequate protection to the institution.

5. Credit limits that consider both settlement and pre-settlement exposures should be established for all counterparties with whom the institution conducts business. As a matter of general policy, business with a counterparty should not commence until a credit line has been approved. The structure of the credit-approval process may differ among institutions, reflecting the organisational and geographic structure of each institution. Nevertheless, in all cases, it is important that credit limits be determined by personnel who are independent of the derivatives function, that these personnel use standards consistent with those used for other activities and that counterparty credit lines are consistent with the organisation's policies and consolidated exposures.

6. If credit limits are exceeded, exceptions should be resolved according to the institution's policies and procedures. In addition, the institution's reports should adequately provide traders and credit officers with relevant, accurate and timely information about the credit exposures and approved credit lines.

7. Similar to bank loans, OTC derivatives products can have credit exposures existing for an extended period. Given these potentially long-term exposures and the complexity associated with some derivatives instruments, an institution should consider the overall financial strength of its counterparties and their ability to perform on their obligations.

Market risk

8. Market risk is the risk to an institution's financial condition resulting from adverse movements in the level or volatility of market prices.

The market risks created – or hedged – by a future or swap are familiar, although not necessarily straightforward to manage. They are exposures to changes in the price of the underlying cash instrument and to changes in interest rates. By contrast, the value of an option is also affected by other factors, including the volatility of the price of the underlying instrument and the passage of time. In addition, all trading activities are affected by market liquidity and by local or world political and economical events.

9. Market risk is increasingly measured by market participants using a value-at-risk approach, which measures the potential gain or loss in a position, portfolio or institution that is associated with a price movement of a given probability over a specified time horizon. The institution should revalue all trading portfolios and calculate its exposures at least daily. Although an institution may use risk measures other than value at risk, the measure used should be sufficiently accurate and rigorous, and the institution should ensure that it is adequately incorporated into its risk-management process.

10. An institution should compare its estimated market risk exposures with actual behaviour. In particular, the output of any market risk models that require simulations or forecasts of future prices should be compared with actual results. If the projected and actual results differ materially, the assumptions used to derive the projections should be carefully reviewed or the models should be modified, as appropriate.

11. The institution should establish limits for market risk that relate to its risk measures and that are consistent with maximum exposures authorised by its senior management and board of directors. These limits should be allocated to business units and individual decision-makers and be clearly understood by all relevant parties. Exceptions to limits should be detected and adequately addressed by management. In practice, some limit systems may include additional elements such as stop-loss limits and guidelines that may play an important role in controlling risks.

12. An institution whose derivatives activities are limited in volume and confined to end-user activities may need less sophisticated risk-measurement systems than those required by a dealer. Senior

management at such an institution should ensure that all significant risks arising from its derivatives transactions can be quantified, monitored and controlled. At a minimum, risk-management systems should evaluate the possible impact on the institution's earnings and capital which may result from adverse changes in interest rates and other market conditions that are relevant to risk exposure and the effectiveness of derivatives transactions in the institution's overall risk management.

Liquidity risk

13. An institution faces two types of liquidity risk in its derivatives activities: one related to specific products or markets and the other related to the general funding of the institution's derivatives activities. The former is the risk that an institution may not be able to, or cannot easily, unwind or offset a particular position at or near the previous market price because of inadequate market depth or because of disruptions in the marketplace. Funding liquidity risk is the risk that the institution will be unable to meet its payment obligations on settlement dates or in the event of margin calls. Because neither type of liquidity risk is necessarily unique to derivatives activities, management should evaluate these risks in the broader context of the institution's overall liquidity. When establishing limits, the institution should be aware of the size, depth and liquidity of the particular market and establish guidelines accordingly.

14. In developing guidelines for controlling liquidity risks, an institution should consider the possibility that it could lose access to one or more markets, either because of concerns about the institution's own creditworthiness, the creditworthiness of a major counterparty or because of generally stressful market conditions. At such times, the institution may have less flexibility in managing its market, credit and liquidity risk exposures. An institution that makes markets in over-the-counter derivatives or that dynamically hedges (dynamic hedging refers generally to the continuous process of buying or selling instruments to offset open exposures as market conditions change (e.g. an option writer selling an underlying asset as its price falls)) its positions requires constant access to financial markets and that need may increase in times of market stress. The institution's liquidity plan

should reflect the institution's ability to turn to alternative markets, such as futures or cash markets, or to provide sufficient collateral or other credit enhancements in order to continue trading under a broad range of scenarios.

15. An institution that participates in over-the-counter derivatives markets should assess the potential liquidity risks associated with the early termination of derivatives contracts. Many forms of standardised contracts for derivatives transactions allow counterparties to request collateral or to terminate their contracts early if the institution experiences an adverse credit event or a deterioration in its financial condition. In addition, under conditions of market stress, customers may ask for the early termination of some contracts within the context of the dealer's market-making activities. In such situations, an institution that owes money on derivatives transactions may be required to deliver collateral or settle a contract early and possibly at a time when the institution may face other funding and liquidity pressures. Early terminations may also open up additional, unintended, market positions. Management and directors should be aware of these potential liquidity risks and should address them in the insitution's liquidity plan and in the broader context of the institution's liquidity management process.

Operations risk

16. Operations risk is the risk that deficiencies in information systems or internal control will result in unexpected loss. This risk is associated with human error, system failures and inadequate procedures and controls. This risk can be exacerbated in the case of certain derivatives because of the complex nature of their payment structures and calculation of their values.

17. The board of directors and senior management should ensure the proper dedication of resources (financial and personnel) to support operations and systems development and maintenance. The operations unit for derivatives activities, consistent with other trading and investment activities, should report to an independent unit and should be managed independently of the business unit. The sophistication of the systems support and operational capacity should be commensurate with the size and complexity of the derivatives business activity.

18. Systems support and operational capacity should be adequate to accommodate the types of derivatives activities in which the institution engages. This includes the ability to efficiently process and settle the volumes transacted through the business unit, to provide support for the complexity of the transactions booked and to provide accurate and timely input. Support systems and the systems developed to interface with the official databases should generate accurate information sufficient to allow business unit management and senior management to monitor risk exposures in a timely manner.

19. Systems needs for derivatives activities should be evaluated during the strategic planning process. Current and projected volumes should be considered together with the nature of the derivatives activity and the user's expectations. Consistent with other systems plans, a written contingency plan for derivatives products should be in place.

20. With the complexity of derivatives products and the size and rapidity of transactions, it is essential that operational units be able to capture all relevant details of transactions, identify errors and process payments or move assets quickly and accurately. This requires a staff of sufficient size, knowledge and experience to support the volume and type of transactions generated by the business unit. Management should develop appropriate hiring practices and compensation plans to recruit and retain high calibre staff.

21. Systems design and needs may vary according to the size and complexity of the derivatives business. However, each system should provide for accurate and timely processing and allow for proper risk exposure monitoring. Operational systems should be tailored to each institution's needs. Limited end-users of derivatives may not require the same degree of automation needed by more active trading institutions. All operational systems and units should adequately provide for basic processing, settlement and control of derivatives transactions.

22. The more sophisticated the institution's activity, the more need there is to establish automated systems to accommodate the complexity and volume of the deals transacted, to report position data accurately and to facilitate efficient reconciliation.

23. Segregation of operational duties, exposure reporting and risk monitoring from the business unit is critical to proper internal con-

trol. Proper internal control should be provided over the entry of transactions into the database, transaction numbering, date and time notation and the conformation and settlement processes. Operational controls should also be in place to resolve disputes over contract specifications. In this regard, an institution must ensure that trades are confirmed as quickly as possible. The institution should monitor the consistency between the terms of a transaction as they were agreed upon and the terms as they were subsequently confirmed.

24. The operations department, or another unit or entity independent of the business unit, should be responsible for ensuring proper reconciliation of front and back office databases on a regular basis. This includes the verification of position data, profit and loss figures and transaction-by-transaction details.

25. The institution should ensure that the methods it uses to value its derivatives positions are appropriate and that the assumptions underlying those methods are reasonable. The pricing procedures and models the institution chooses should be consistently applied and well documented. Models and supporting statistical analyses should be validated prior to use and as market conditions warrant.

26. Management of the institution should ensure that a mechanism exists whereby derivatives contract documentation is confirmed, maintained and safeguarded. An institution should establish a process through which documentation exceptions are monitored and resolved and appropriately reviewed by senior management and legal counsel. The institution should also have approved policies that specify documentation requirements for derivatives activities and formal procedures for saving and safeguarding important documents that are consistent with legal requirements and internal policies.

27. Although operations risks are difficult to quantify, they can often be evaluated by examining a series of 'worst-case' or 'what-if' scenarios, such as a power loss, a doubling of transaction volume or a mistake found in the pricing software for collateral management. They can also be assessed through periodic reviews of procedures, documentation requirements, data processing systems, contingency plans and other operational practices. Such reviews may help to reduce the likelihood of errors and breakdowns in controls, improve the control of risk

and the effectiveness of the limit system and prevent unsound marketing practices and the premature adoption of new products or lines of business. Considering the heavy reliance of derivatives activities on computerised systems, an institution must have plans that take into account potential problems with its normal processing procedures.

Legal risk

28. Legal risk is the risk that contracts are not legally enforceable or documented correctly. Legal risks should be limited and managed through policies developed by the institution's legal counsel (typically in consultation with officers in the risk-management process) that have been approved by the institution's senior management and board of directors. At a minimum, there should be guidelines and processes in place to ensure the enforceability of counterparty agreements.

29. Prior to engaging in derivatives transactions, an institution should reasonably satisfy itself that its counterparties have the legal and necessary regulatory authority to engage in those transactions. In addition to determining the authority of a counterparty to enter into a derivatives transaction, an institution should also reasonably satisfy itself that the terms of any contract governing its derivatives activities with a counterparty are legally sound.

30. An institution should adequately evaluate the enforceability of its agreements before individual transactions are consummated. Participants in the derivatives markets have experienced significant losses because they were unable to recover losses from defaulting counterparty when a court held the counterparty had acted outside of its authority in entering into such transactions. An institution should ensure that its counterparties have the power and authority to enter into derivatives transactions and that the counterparties' obligations arising from them are enforceable. Similarly, an institution should also ensure that its rights with respect to any margin or collateral received from a counterparty are enforceable and exercisable.

31. The advantages of netting arrangements can include a reduction in credit and liquidity risks, the potential to do more business with existing counterparties within existing credit lines and a reduced need for collateral to support counterparty obligations. The institution should

ascertain that its netting agreements are adequately documented and that they have been executed properly. Only when a netting arrangement is legally enforceable in all relevant jurisdictions should an institution monitor its credit and liquidity risks on a net basis.

APPENDIX III

The Derivatives Policy Group's management controls proposals

The Derivatives Policy Group report is divided into four principal categories:

- management controls;
- enhanced reporting;
- evaluation of risk in relation to capital;
- counterparty relationships.

Under management controls – its key area – the report makes a number of proposals, which are reproduced below.

Outline of risk-management controls

Firms engaged in significant OTC derivatives activities should have in place comprehensive internal risk-management control systems that are commensurate with the scope, size and complexity of the activities that have been authorised and the nature and extent of the risks they entail. The following overview summarises the key elements of such risk-management control systems.

A. Certain definitions

1. *Risk* References in this discussion to risk encompass the following:

- *market risk*: the risk that a change in liquidity or in the level of one or more market prices, rates, indices, volatilities, correlations or other market factors will result in losses for a specified position or portfolio;
- *credit risk*: the risk that a counterparty will fail to perform its obligations to the firm;

- *liquidity risk*: the risk that, as a result of mismatches in the timing of cash inflows and outflows, a firm will have inadequate cash available to fund current obligations;
- *legal risk*: the risk that a counterparty's performance obligations will be unenforceable because (i) the underlying transaction documentation is inadequate; (ii) the counterparty lacks the requisite authority or is subject to legal transaction restrictions; (iii) the underlying transaction is impermissible under applicable law; or (iv) applicable bankruptcy or insolvency laws limit or alter contractual remedies; and
- *operational risk*: the risk of human error or deficiencies in the firm's operating systems (e.g. database management, trade entry, trade processing, trade confirmation, payment, delivery, receipt, collateral management, valuation and related information systems).

2. *Risk monitoring* Risk monitoring is that function within a firm that identifies, measures, monitors and reports on the market, credit and liquidity risks incurred by the firm.

3. *Risk management* Risk management is that process within a firm by which risk guidelines are established, allocated and managed.

B. Role of the governing body or other authorising body

1. *Authorising Body* The OTC derivatives activities of a firm should be conducted pursuant to general authorising guidelines (*Authorising Guidelines*) reviewed and approved by the firm's governing body (i.e. a board of directors or its equivalent), a committee of such governing body or a committee designated by the governing body for the purpose of approving such guidelines (*Authorising Body*). The Authorising Body should be selected by the governing body based on, among other relevant considerations, the composition and expertise of the governing body, the customary allocation of equivalent responsibilities within senior management of the firm and the nature, scope and complexity of the firm's OTC derivatives activities.

   If the Authorising Body is not the governing body (or a committee comprised exclusively of members of the governing body) of the firm the Authorising Guidelines, and material amendments to the

Authorising Guidelines, should be reported to the firm's governing body (or a committee comprised exclusively of members of the governing body).

2. *Written guidelines* The Authorising Guidelines should be adopted in written form by the firm's Authorising Body.

3. *Relevant considerations* Relevant factors to be considered by the Authorising Body in approving Authorising Guidelines include the firm's overall business strategies and product lines, its tolerance for risk and its general risk-management philosophy, its past performance and experience, its financial condition and capital levels, its internal expertise and experience, the sophistication of its risk-monitoring and risk-management systems and processes and any regulatory or organisational, constraints.

4. *Authorising Guidelines* The Authorising Guidelines should address the following areas:

   - the scope, or the procedures for determining the scope, of authorised activity or any non-quantitative limitation on the scope of authorised activities;
   - the quantitative guidelines for managing the firm's overall or constituent risk exposure(s);
   - the significant structural elements of the firm's risk-monitoring and risk-management systems and processes;
   - the scope and frequency of reporting by management on risk exposures; and
   - the mechanisms for reviewing the Authorising Guidelines.

   (a) *Scope of authorised activity* If the Authorising Body wishes to impose specific (non-quantitative) constraints on the scope of permitted activities (such as product, market, geographic or trading strategy restrictions), the Authorising Guidelines should specify any restrictions. If the Authorising Body wishes to approve only specific activities, the Authorising Guidelines should specify the scope of authorised activity. The Authorising Guidelines may designate one or more individuals within management or management committees to perform the function of authorising or restricting activities in particular products or markets.

(b) *Guidelines on risk exposure(s)* The Authorising Guidelines should establish market and credit risk exposure guidelines applicable to the overall or constituent risk exposure(s) of the firm's derivatives activities. Risk exposure guidelines should be based on factors such as the character of the risk(s) being measured, the extent and nature of the derivative products utilised, the risk-measurement methodology employed by the firm and the nature of the firm's counterparties and their industry, country or credit rating categories.

If the Authorising Guidelines do not contain specific limits on risk exposures, they should contain quantitative guidelines sufficient to enable management to implement specific quantitative limits. The Authorising Guidelines may provide that specified individuals or committees within management, independent from or senior to the relevant business or trading unit, may approve exceptions to the quantitative guidelines in the Authorising Guidelines, with material exceptions to be periodically reported to the Authorising Body.

The Authorising Guidelines should also address the degree to which the firm's OTC derivatives-related risk exposures should be aggregated, for purposes of risk monitoring and risk management, with the related risk exposures arising from other trading activities of the firm.

(c) *Risk-monitoring and risk-management structures* The Authorising Guidelines should address the following structural elements of risk monitoring and risk management:

1. *An independent process and checks and balances for risk monitoring.* The Authorising Guidelines should define a process for risk monitoring independent from the business or trading units whose activities create the risks being monitored.

   In connection with risk-monitoring systems, the Authorising Body should also consider the need for organisational checks and balances to protect against irregularities or inconsistencies in risk measurement and to ensure to the greatest extent practicable that the risks posed by OTC derivative (and related) products are uniformly and accurately identified and evaluated.

2. *The appropriate degree of independence for risk management.* The Authorising Guidelines should define a risk-management function to be performed by specified committees or individuals independent from or senior to the relevant business or trading units whose activities create risks for the firm.

3. *Authority, resources and information reporting.* The Authorising Body should determine that the bodies or personnel performing risk-monitoring and risk-management functions have the necessary authority and resources to accomplish their management control objectives. The Authorising Body should also determine that mechanisms are in place through which information regarding the firm's risk-creating activities will be reported to risk-monitoring and risk-management personnel.

4. *Ongoing review of systems and processes.* The Authorising Body should review from time to time the firm's risk-monitoring and risk-management systems and processes.

5. *Scope and frequency of reporting.* The Authorising Guidelines should identify the type, scope and frequency of reports to be prepared in connection with the firm's risk-monitoring and risk-management systems and processes and to be made available for review by the governing body, the Authorising Body and senior management. Such reports should contain information regarding the firm's positions and risk exposures to facilitate effective oversight of the risk-monitoring and risk-management functions. The Authorising Body should review the scope and frequency of reporting as business and market circumstances change.

C. Role of management

Firm management should ensure that control procedures with respect to the firm's OTC derivatives activities are consistent with the firm's Authorising Guidelines, including, in particular, procedures with respect to the following matters:

1. *Measurement of risk consistent with prescribed guidelines* Systems and procedures should be in place to identify and assess the mater-

ial risks arising from the firm's OTC derivatives activities and to assist in managing those risks.

Risk identification and measurement procedures should address the following risk factors.

(a) *Market risk* Mechanisms should be in place to measure market risk consistent with established risk-measurement guidelines. These procedures should include the capability to measure (to the extent material in light of the character of the firm's portfolio) basic components of market risk on a business unit (or, if desired, trading strategy) level as well as on a firm-wide level and to provide the information necessary to conduct 'stress testing'.

(b) *Credit risk* Procedures should be in place to measure the risk that a counterparty will be unable to meet its obligations to the firm and to measure credit exposures and concentrations against established guidelines (e.g. guidelines based on counterparty or on industry, country or credit rating category). Credit risk-measurement systems should assess both the firm's current credit exposure to a counterparty (i.e. the current market value or replacement cost of the transaction) and its potential exposure (i.e. the firm's risk of additional exposure to the counterparty due to possible future changes in applicable market rates, prices or levels during the term of the transaction).

Management should consider the use of risk-reducing practices such as bilateral and multilateral netting arrangements, collateral agreements, third-party credit enhancements and offsetting exposures to the same counterparty.

(c) *Liquidity risk* Procedures should be in place to measure and provide for potential funding requirements that might arise as a result of the impact of market movements on cash flows and collateral and margin requirements in light of mismatches in the timing of offsetting payment and delivery obligations, taking into account the potential impact of contractual provisions, such as early termination provisions, that may give rise to such timing mismatches.

2. *Establishment of risk guidelines for business units* Market risk exposure guidelines should be in place for each of the firm's business units.

3. *Data collection and synthesis* Processes should be in place through which the data necessary to conduct risk-monitoring and risk-management functions effectively is made readily accessible on a timely basis and information management systems are available to capture, monitor, analyse and report relevant data.

4. *Policies for valuation methodology* Systems and procedures should be in place to mark to market the value of OTC derivative products or portfolios accurately and on a timely basis, as necessary to implement the risk-monitoring and risk-management functions required under the Authorising Guidelines.

   The firm's valuation systems should identify and utilise definitions of value (e.g. mid-market or replacement cost) in view of the particular OTC derivative products or markets involved and the purposes for which the valuation is used, and techniques should be identified to address situations where no market prices are readily observable. Valuation data collected with respect to an instrument or portfolio should be documented, should specify any pricing or related assumptions and should be maintained for review by the firm's auditors or other authorised examiners.

   (a) *Frequency of mark to market* The frequency with which derivatives positions or portfolios are required to be marked to market should be consistent with the risk-management guidelines established by the Authorising Body and should be based on the volatility of the relevant market factor(s) and the nature of the firm's risk profile.

   (b) *Valuation policy* A valuation policy should be in place that reflects fair market value and, where appropriate, incorporates adjustments for credit quality, market liquidity, funding costs and transaction administration costs.

   (c) *Pricing verification procedures* Routine procedures should be in place, where practicable, for verifying the prices assigned to particular OTC derivative products. In addition, procedures and parameters should be in place for validating valuation methodologies on a periodic basis. Any assumptions (such as historic correlations and volatilities) used in such valuations should be periodically evaluated.

(d) *Model verification procedures* Statistical or other simulation models for conducting 'stress tests' and measuring the impact of various market movements on the value of OTC derivative products or portfolios should themselves be subject to review and validation. Among other objectives, such review and validation should compare model predictions against actual market performances and should provide for timely identification and correction of any deficiencies in the models.

5. *Establish a process for identifying and managing deviations from risk guidelines* A method should be in place for identifying and reviewing situations in which internal risk-management guidelines have been exceeded and for taking any responsive or remedial action that may be necessary.

6. *Other controls* Other management control functions include the following.

(a) *Legal risk* Procedures should be in place to monitor and address the risk that an OTC derivative transaction will be unenforceable because (i) the underlying transaction documentation is inadequate; (ii) the counterparty lacks the requisite authority or is subject to legal transaction restrictions; (iii) the underlying transaction is impermissible under applicable law; or (iv) applicable bankruptcy or insolvency laws limit or alter contractual remedies.

(b) *Operational risk* Procedures should be in place to adequately identify and address any deficiencies in the firm's operating systems (e.g. database management, trade entry, trade processing, trade confirmation, payment, delivery, receipt, collateral management, valuation and related information systems) and to contain the extent of losses arising from unidentified deficiencies. Operational risk measurement and management procedures should, as appropriate, also incorporate the use of disaster recovery planning or related techniques for reducing the firm's exposure to operational risks.

(c) *Designate authority to commit on trades* Procedures should be in place to authorise certain employees to commit the firm to particular types of derivatives transactions, to specify any quantitative limits on such authority and to provide for the oversight of their exercise of such authority. Authorised employees should understand the risk exposures arising from the product in question, the applicable risk-management guidelines and the management control procedures for documenting, recording and reporting the transaction.

(d) *Role of external audit functions* External auditors should periodically review the integrity of risk-monitoring and risk-management functions.

(e) *Approve internal controls for documentation, adequacy of operational procedures and risk-reduction procedures* Procedures should be in place to provide for adequate documentation of the principal terms of OTC derivatives transactions and other relevant information regarding such transactions. Such documentation should be appropriately maintained and should be made available to the firm's auditors or other authorised examiners. Internal operational systems should also provide for effective tracking and processing of OTC derivatives transactions from their initiation to their settlement.

(f) *Provide for an adequate level of professional expertise for risk monitoring and risk management* Adequate personnel resources with appropriate expertise should be committed to implementing effectively the firm's risk-monitoring and risk-management systems and processes.

INDEX

Dear Pitman Publishing Customer

IMPORTANT – Please Read This Now!

We are delighted to announce a special free service for all of our customers.

Simply complete this form and return it to the FREEPOST address overleaf to receive:

A Free Customer Newsletter

B Free Information Service

C Exclusive Customer Offers – which have included free software, videos and relevant products

D Opportunity to take part in product development sessions

E The chance for you to write about your own business experience and become one of our respected authors

Fill this in now and return it to us (no stamp needed in the UK) to join our customer information service.

Name: Position:

Company/Organisation:

Address (including postcode):

Country:

Telephone: Fax:

Nature of business:

Title of book purchased:

ISBN (printed on back cover): 0 2 7 3 ☐☐☐☐☐ ☐

Comments:

---------- Fold Here Then Staple Once ----------

We would be very grateful if you could answer these questions to help us with market research.

1 Where/How did you hear of this book?

- ☐ in a bookshop
- ☐ in a magazine/newspaper (please state which):
- ☐ information through the post
- ☐ recommendation from a colleague
- ☐ other (please state which):

2 Where did you buy this book

- ☐ Direct from Pitman Publishing
- ☐ From a bookclub
- ☐ From a bookshop (state which)

3 Which newspaper(s)/magazine(s) do you read regularly?:

4 When buying a business book which factors influence you most?

(Please rank in order)

- ☐ recommendation from a colleague
- ☐ price
- ☐ content
- ☐ recommendation in a bookshop
- ☐ author
- ☐ publisher
- ☐ title
- ☐ other(s):

5 Is this book a

- ☐ personal purchase?
- ☐ company purchase?

6 Would you be prepared to spend a few minutes talking to our customer services staff to help with product development? YES/NO

We occasionally make our customer lists available to companies whose products or services we feel may be of interest. If you do not want this service write 'exclude from other mailings' on this card. The Customer Information Service is liable to change without notice.